Start Your Own

SENIOR SERVICES BUSINESS

Additional titles in *Entrepreneur's* Startup Series

Start Your Own

Arts and Crafts Business

Automobile Detailing Business

Bar and Club

Bed and Breakfast

Blogging Business

Business on eBay

Car Wash

Child-Care Service

Cleaning Service

Clothing Store and More

Coaching Business

Coin-Operated Laundry

Construction and Contracting Business

Consulting Business

Day Spa and More

e-Business

Event Planning Business

Executive Recruiting Business

Fashion Accessories Business

Florist Shop and Other Floral Businesses

Food Truck Business

Freelance Writing Business and More

Freight Brokerage Business

Gift Basket Service

Grant-Writing Business

Graphic Design Business

Green Business

Hair Salon and Day Spa

Home Inspection Service

Import/Export Business

Information Marketing Business

Kid-Focused Business

Lawn Care or Landscaping Business

Mail Order Business

Medical Claims Billing Service

Net Services Business

Online Coupon or Daily Deal Business

Online Education Business

Personal Concierge Service

Personal Training Business

Pet Business and More

Pet-Sitting Business and More

Photography Business

Public Relations Business

Restaurant and More

Retail Business and More

Self-Publishing Business

Seminar Production Business

Senior Services Business

Travel Business and More

Tutoring and Test Prep Business

Vending Business

Wedding Consultant Business

Wholesale Distribution Business

Entrepreneur
MAGAZINE'S

startup

Start Your Own

3RD EDITION

SENIOR
SERVICES
BUSINESS

Adult Day-Care ◆ *Relocation Service*
Home-Care ◆ *Transportation Service*
Concierge ◆ *Travel Service*

Entrepreneur Press and Charlene Davis

EP
Entrepreneur
PRESS®

Entrepreneur Press, Publisher
Cover Design: Beth Hansen-Winter
Production and Composition: Eliot House Productions

This publication is designed to provide accurate and authoritative information in regard to
the subject matter covered. It is sold with the understanding that the publisher is not
engaged in rendering legal, accounting or other professional services. If legal advice or other
expert assistance is required, the services of a competent professional person should be
sought.

Library of Congress Cataloging-in-Publication Data
Davis, Charlene, 1957–
Start your own senior services business: your step-by-step guide to success/by
Entrepreneur Press and Charlene Davis.
    pages cm. — (Start your own)
    Revised edition of the authors' Start your own senior services business: adult day-care,
relocation service, home-care, transportation service, concierge, travel service and more,
2nd ed.
    ISBN-10: 1-59918-541-5 (paperback)
    ISBN-13: 978-1-59918-541-5 (paperback)
    1. Older people—Services for—United States—Handbooks, manuals, etc. 2. Adult day
care centers—United States—Handbooks, manuals, etc. 3. Retirees—Services for—United
States—Handbooks, manuals, etc. 4. New business enterprises—United States—Handbooks, manuals, etc. I. Entrepreneur Press. II. Title.
    HQ1064.U5L95 2014
    362.6'30973—dc23   2014017894

Printed in the United States of America

18 17 16 15 14   10 9 8 7 6 5 4 3 2 1

Contents

▲

▲

▲

Preface

During the next 25 years, the senior population in America is expected to double from 35 million to 71.5 million, creating an ever-growing need for quality senior services. There has never been a better time to target the 65+ demographic, which is a large, lucrative, and quickly growing market. This need is producing tremendous opportunities for savvy entrepreneurs who are recognizing that now is the time to carve a niche in the senior market.

Businesses that focus on senior services can range from small homebased operations to large commercial enterprises, and can be started with an investment of as little as a few hundred dollars. Your business can remain a small, one-person operation or grow into a significantly larger enterprise bringing in potentially millions of dollars in revenue.

One of the neat things about owning your own business is that you are the boss (aka head honcho, top dog, big cheese). The good news is that you get to sign the checks. The bad news is that you have to sign the checks. You also can't call in sick or defer to someone to a higher authority. But it's all good because we're going to help you get on top of your game with sage advice from successful entrepreneurs, worksheets to help estimate expenses and operating costs, nitty-gritty details about the senior industry, and much more.

Let's start with some standard business advice which is to define and know your market. If you enjoy working with older people, that could well be the easiest part of starting a business serving seniors, because this is a market that is easy to identify and reach and much in need of your services.

This guide also explores some of more prevalent lifestyle options members of the older generation will want to have as they move through their retirement years. We're going to look at senior business ventures involving concierge services, transportation, travel, relocation services, homecare and home health-care, and senior adult day-care operations.

So relax, start reading, and explore all of the options that will soon get you on the fast track to success.

Serving
Seniors

The trends reveal an abundance of new opportunities for entrepreneurs who want to combine caring with nurturing. Baby boomers—members of the generation born between 1946 and 1964—have already started receiving Social Security retirement benefits, and the U.S. Census Bureau

▲

estimates the 65 and older demographic will grow faster than the total population in every state. The National Association of Area Agencies on Aging estimates by the year 2030, one in five people in the United States will be over the age of 65. The elderly population is increasing at nearly twice the rate of the general population—the 85-plus segment is projected to swell to about 19 million by 2050.

The evolving needs of older generations are having a major influence on what resources are necessary to prepare for the social and economic impact of the "senior boom." Considering starting a business serving this market? Then you must know how urgent the need is for senior services. Jacqueline (Jacke) S. Dollar of Easy Aging, Geriatric Case Management Services, says that national demographics demonstrate the need for a variety of senior services. "Most seniors want to age-in-place in their own homes," she says. "Today's boomers are interested in engaging in their own retirement and are willing to pay for a professional to assist their parents."

As people grow older, their needs and lifestyles change. There comes a time when even healthy, able-bodied seniors want to move from their larger homes into smaller ones that are easier to care for, or they may consider retirement communities. As their physical abilities naturally decline, seniors who want to stay in their own homes look for outside assistance with daily tasks, such as preparing meals, housekeeping, and managing personal hygiene. Seniors who are no longer able to drive may seek out reliable transportation to medical appointments, social functions, or shopping expeditions. And when seniors are no longer able to live alone, they may move in with family members or relocate to assisted living facilities. Almost 6.5 million seniors currently need assistance with their daily activities, and this number is expected to double by 2020.

On the other hand, seniors are healthier now than people of the same age were 30 years ago. Wellness for seniors has become an important issue in our society. As human longevity increases, there is a keen desire to remain healthy and independent for as long as possible. These active seniors have time on their hands and disposable income in the bank, and many want to travel to interesting and exotic places.

Tom Mann of TR Mann Consulting (TRMann.com), a full-service marketing and advertising agency that specializes in the senior market says the opportunities for working with the mature market are staggering. Between 2012 and 2060, the population aged 65 and older is expected to more than double from 43.1 million to 92.0 million. "When you consider these are the people who hold the bulk of the country's money and are undergoing significant life changes, it becomes clear that they will drive the lion's share of our economy," he says.

All these trends mean opportunity for savvy entrepreneurs who want to start businesses serving this lucrative and growing market. Senior relocation specialists help their older clients with moving and downsizing. Home care, home health-care, and senior day-care operations all provide services to help people live at home for as long

Stat Fact
According to the Administration on Aging (aoa.gov), the older population—persons 65 years or older—numbered 35.6 million in 2009, representing 12.9 percent of the U.S. population, or about one in every eight Americans. By 2030, there will be about 72.1 million older persons, more than twice their number in 2000.

as possible. And a travel agent who specializes in making arrangements for seniors is just the ticket to send them off on a fun-filled adventure.

Dollar advises entrepreneurs to research what's already available in the community and decide how you and your senior service will be better, different, and provide a niche not already met. "Start slowly," she says. "Have a mentor who's been in practice for several years and keep your day job until you're profitable."

When you serve seniors, you typically wear many hats—and often more than one at a time. We'll help you discover the ones that fit the best by showing you how to design a business that complements your talents and your demographics.

You may already know what type of senior services business you want to start, or you may still be exploring your options. In this guide you'll find the information and tools you need to start a senior adult day-care center, a senior relocation business, a home care or home health-care business, a senior concierge service, a senior transportation service, or a senior travel service.

We'll start with an overview of the market, look at the specific services you'll want to consider offering, and then go through the step-by-step process of setting up and running your new venture. You'll learn about basic requirements and startup costs, daily operations, and what to do when things don't go according to plan. We'll discuss how to find, hire, and keep good employees. Plus, you'll gain a solid understanding of the sales and marketing process, as well as how to track and manage the financial side of your business.

The best way to read this book is from beginning to end, and don't skip any chapters—even if you feel some may not apply to you or the type of business you want to start. For example, you may decide that you want to zero in on senior transportation, but if you also read the chapter on senior adult day-care businesses, you may find some good ideas on how to interact and network with those centers. Or you may decide to blend one or two of the concierge services with your senior relocation or travel business.

Stat Fact
As part of their retirement planning, many of today's middle-aged baby boomers are "unretiring" by starting businesses that they intend to sell in 10 to 20 years. They plan to use the revenue from the sale of their company as retirement income.

What you won't learn is how to get rich quick or become an overnight success. Being an entrepreneur requires hard work, dedication, and commitment. In addition, working with seniors can be challenging; it requires empathy, patience and understanding of their special needs. But it can also be tremendously rewarding—monetarily and personally—as you discover what a tremendous difference you can make in someone's life.

The Pros and Cons of Franchising

Franchising can be a great way to start a new business because even though you are in business for yourself, you're not alone. You can start your new venture with a proven working model, an enthusiastic team of go-getters, and comprehensive hands-on training.

Here's How It Works

In a nutshell, the franchisor lends his trademark or trade name and a business model to the franchisee, who pays a royalty and often an initial fee for the right to do business under the franchisor's name and system. The contract binding the two parties is the franchise, but that term is also used to describe the business the franchisee operates.

The best part is the franchisor has already worked the kinks out of the system and is available to help franchisees when new challenges arise. According to the Small Business Administration, most businesses fail from lack of management skills. This is less likely to happen with a franchised business, because your franchisor is there to guide you through the maze of business ownership.

Typically you think of fast food and restaurants when you think of franchising, but virtually every business form has the potential to be franchised, and there are a number of franchised businesses that target seniors. In fact, once your business is established, you may want to consider growing it by franchising your concept.

Here Are the Cons

While there are many benefits to owning a franchise (security, training, and marketing power), there are some drawbacks. Perhaps the most significant is the cost of a franchise. The initial franchise fee can run anywhere from a few thousand to several hundred thousand dollars. Then you have continuing royalty payments to the franchisor which are based on the weekly or monthly gross income of your business. Additional expenses may include promotional and advertising fees, operating licenses and permits, insurance, and other costs of running a business.

Stat Fact

A recent study conducted by PricewaterhouseCoopers, found that the franchising sector generates 18 million jobs in the United States alone and yields $1.53 trillion in economic output.

Another big drawback is that you have to give up some of your independence. Each franchise is different with how firm their conditions and requirements are; however, you will be bound by the contract to follow and implement the rules and procedures established by the franchisor. For example, if you neglect to pay your royalty fees or misbehave by not meeting performance standards, your franchise could be terminated and you may lose your investment. So, if you like to make your own decisions and "do your own thing," a franchise may not be right for you.

Before You Buy

Doing your homework before buying a franchise is essential. You'll be making a huge financial commitment, so you need to be sure the business suits you.

The International Franchise Association recommends that you investigate the following points:

○ The type of experience required
○ The business itself (you need a complete understanding of it)
○ The hours and personal commitment necessary to run the business
○ Who the franchisor is, what its track record has been, and the business experience of its officers and directors
○ How other franchisees in the same system are doing
○ How much the startup costs are (the franchise fee and other startup costs)
○ How much you're going to pay for the continuing right to operate the business (royalties)
○ If there are any products or services you must buy from the franchisor, and how and by whom they are supplied
○ The terms and conditions under which the franchise relationship can be terminated or renewed, and how many franchisees have left the system during the past few years
○ The financial condition of the franchisor

You also have no control over how the franchisor operates, and the corporate office can make decisions that you may not agree with or that may even reduce your profitability. That's why it's so important to thoroughly research a franchise; you want to see a positive operational pattern before making a commitment.

Much of the information you'll need about a franchise will be provided in the form of a document known as the UFOC, or Uniform Franchise Offering Circular. Under Federal Trade Commission (FTC) rules, you must receive this document at least 10 business days before you are asked to sign any contract or pay any money to the franchisor.

Buying an Existing Business

An alternative to buying a franchise or to starting your own senior services business is to take over an existing operation. It may seem like an attractive and simple shortcut to skip the work involved in building a business from scratch and get started in an operation that's already equipped and generating revenue, but you should approach this option with caution.

You'll find a variety of businesses for sale advertised in trade publications, local newspapers, and through business brokers. The businesses can often be purchased lock, stock, and barrel, including equipment, office supplies, and existing clients.

Of course, there are drawbacks to buying a business. Though the actual dollar amounts required depend on the size and type of business, it often takes more cash to buy an existing business than to start one yourself. When you buy a company's assets, you usually get stuck with at least some of its liabilities, as well. And it's highly unlikely that you'll find an existing business that is precisely the company you would have built on your own. Even so, you just might find the business you want is owned by someone else.

Why do people sell businesses—especially profitable ones? There are a variety of reasons. Many entrepreneurs are happiest during the startup and early growth stages of a company; once the business is running smoothly, they get bored and begin looking for something new. Other business owners may grow tired of the responsibility or be facing health or other personal issues that motivate them to sell their companies. They may just be ready to retire and want to turn their hard work into cash for their golden years. In fact, some of the most successful entrepreneurs go into business with a solid plan for how they're going to get out of the business when the time comes.

Smart Tip

If you buy an existing business, include a non-compete clause in your sales contract. Your new business won't be worth much if the seller opens a competing operation down the street a few weeks after you take over the old company.

It's also possible that the business is for sale because it has problems—and while they may not stop you from buying it, you should know all the details before you make a decision. The following steps will help you:

- *Find out why the business is for sale.* Don't accept what the current owner says at face value; do some research to make an independent confirmation.
- *Examine the business's financial records for the previous three years and for the current year-to-date.* Compare tax records with the owner's claims of revenue and profits.
- *Spend a few days observing the operation.* For example, if you're looking at a home care or home health-care service, ride along with one or two aides. If you're considering an adult day-care, sit in at the facility for a few hours a day for several days.
- *Speak with current clients.* Are they satisfied with the service? Are they willing to give a new owner a chance? Ask for their input, both positive and negative, and ask what you can do to improve the operation. Remember, even though sales volume and cash flow may be a primary reason for buying an existing business, customers are under no obligation to stay with you when you take over.
- *Consider hiring someone skilled in business acquisitions to assist you in negotiating the sale price and terms of the deal.*
- *Remember that you can walk away from the deal at any point in the negotiation process before a contract is signed.*

Starting Your Own Business

It may be that your best path to business ownership is starting a senior services company yourself, and that's what this book is all about. Let's start by taking a look at what it's like to be in the business of serving seniors.

Running Your
Senior Care
Service

Most people start a particular type of business because they enjoy doing that kind of work, and the typical owner of a senior services business is no different. You may find it frustrating that a major portion of your time will be spent on tasks other than doing work for your clients. In fact, it won't be unusual for you to have days that are extremely busy and you work very hard, but you don't have interactions with clients.

As a solo operator, expect to spend at least one-fourth of your time on general business management and administration, marketing, purchasing, and billing. The bigger your business and the more workers you have, the more time you'll spend managing them instead of doing the work yourself. By contrast, the smaller your operation, the more likely you'll be doing much of the actual work as well as running the company.

For example, the owner of a small senior concierge or relocation business will typically spend a substantial amount of time working closely with clients and coordinating services. Operating a home care (typically nonmedical services) or home health-care business will often mean limited client interaction, because usually the business owner is responsible for supervising a staff of qualified caregivers who are assigned to clients according to their needs.

No matter how small or large your company is, it's critical that you not neglect the administrative side. It won't do you much good if you do the work but never bother to issue invoices so you get paid. Poorly maintained records can get you into trouble with the IRS and other government agencies. Sloppy purchasing procedures can mean you run out of important supplies at critical times. And if you aren't marketing on a regular basis—even when you've got all the work you can handle—your business will eventually dry up.

Although you must pay attention to the business side of your company, you can still design an operation that lets you spend most of your time on tasks you enjoy.

Startup Stories

While it is true that you learn things by doing them, another way to learn something new is by example. After all, there's no reason you should repeat the mistakes of others if they're willing to tell you about them first. Throughout the book, you'll hear from our featured entrepreneurs who have started their own senior service businesses. These folks have built successful careers and have invaluable insights to share with you.

Let's start with Dick Padgett, founder and owner of Five Star Concierge in San Diego. Padgett started his senior concierge service as a transportation and shopping business in 1998, after he realized how much his wife's grandmother needed someone to drive her on errands and to doctor's appointments. Since then, customer demand drove him to expand his operation to include handyman services and personal errands.

Anya Clowers is a registered nurse, travel expert, and speaker who educates travelers about the practical and medical side of travel through her business, Jet With Comfort. "I have found that active seniors are the biggest fans of this topic," she says. Her seminars include one-hour Power Point presentations that teach senior adults how to travel self-sufficiently and "pack peace of mind" by educating them on travel insurance and medical evacuation, the importance of hydration while traveling, how to prevent blood clots, and traveling with diabetes.

After working in rehabilitation massage for six years in the Phoenix, Arizona, area, one of Candy Malburg's clients recommended her to an activity director for a local retirement community. After talking with other activity directors in the area, reading a lot of books, and doing online research, Malburg took additional courses in geriatric massage and began working with senior residents. It wasn't long before she expanded her business to include a total of five retirement communities and two assisted-living communities. Malburg says that working with seniors now makes up 75 to 85 percent of her business.

Karen Martin, owner and founder of Life Moves, LLC, in Hartford, Connecticut, started her moving management service approximately 15 years ago. A realtor friend knew of her nursing background and expertise in antiques and collectibles. She asked Martin for her assistance with an elderly couple who had health concerns and needed to liquidate about 70 percent of their possessions. Recognizing the need for these types of services, Martin launched her business to help seniors who were in transition because of a decline in health, the death of a partner or spouse, or a desire for a change in living arrangements. In 2004, Martin quadrupled her profits from the previous year, indicating how big a need there was for this type of service—especially with seniors.

As the moving management part of Martin's business began slowing down due the economic collapse of the real estate market in 2007–08, Martin added a new "Health Services" division to Life Moves by becoming a patient advocate for seniors. "I accompany my clients to their doctor appointments, explain the medical visits, and follow up with instructions to them and family members," she says. Because she is a Registered Nurse, she is able to dispense medication, provide post-operative care, and comfort measures as needed.

Judy Heft of Stamford, Connecticut, started her business in the mid '90s to assist seniors with paying their bills and other administrative tasks. "I love working with seniors," she says. "Sometimes they are reluctant to ask their children for help since they don't want them to think they are incapable of handling their own affairs. Other times they are just lonely and want someone to talk to and assist them with daily money management." Heft recognized more than a decade ago that the older population was growing significantly and knew there would be a huge need for her services. She feels the most important thing an individual should know or do before starting a senior service business is that seniors want to be treated with respect and don't want to be told they are too old to do things.

A few years ago, Doug Iannelli simultaneously started two senior service businesses: Flying Companions and Appointment Companions. After a friend suffered from a bad stroke, he saw the need to provide disabled and older travelers with nonmedical assistance, as well as accompany seniors to appointments. "My friend had no family in the area and she needed to make arrangements to fly from one state to another for special treatment, but couldn't go alone," Iannelli says. "She also needed help getting to and from doctor appointments around Atlanta." This caused Iannelli to start thinking about other individuals and families in similar situations who needed to get loved ones from one place to another. He knew with baby boomers starting to morph into senior citizens and an increasingly aging population, more and more people would be in need of assistance with appointments and traveling.

In contrast to the aforementioned homebased operations, Allen Hager started his nonmedical home-care business, Right at Home, in 1995 with 20 employees in Omaha, Nebraska. He had worked in the health-care industry for many years and kept seeing what he calls a "care gap." This gap consists of people who fall in between healthy and needing institutional health care; they require only a little assistance to remain independent and in their homes. Because of the demand for these types of services, his operation quickly evolved into a franchise system that now supports more than 2,500 employees.

Diane Ross was already operating a thriving business in Reno, Nevada, when she added adult day care to the mix 18 years ago. Her center, The Continuum, offered a rehabilitation program with physical, occupational, and speech therapy for all ages, a child-care and preschool program, and a home safety evaluation program. The rapid growth of the senior segment in Reno, Nevada, prompted Ross to expand her offerings to meet the needs of that market.

Do You Have What It Takes?

It takes a special type of person to work with seniors. "You have to be a people person and have very good judgment in dealing with people and the issues surrounding them," Hager says. "Whether you are working with clients, caregivers, family members, or with the professionals who are referring you the business, there is going to be very intense people contact." While many of your clients will be able-bodied and lucid, others will suffer from infirmities and varying degrees of dementia. In addition to strong management and entrepreneurial skills, if you plan to work directly with seniors, you need:

- *Honesty and integrity*. You may be trusted with access to your clients' homes and sometimes even to their bank accounts.
- *Patience*. Even the sweetest, best-natured client will have a bad day, and you need sufficient patience to work through it.
- *Versatility*. Often, providing services for seniors necessitates wearing more than one hat at a time. Be flexible and willing to shift gears at a moment's notice.
- *Interpersonal skills*. You need to enjoy being around seniors and not be bashful about making conversation. At the same time, you need to be a good listener. Many seniors like to reminisce about earlier times in their lives, and they have some truly interesting stories to tell.
- *Reliability and punctuality*. Your clients will appreciate being able to depend on you to pick them up on time or keep appointments as promised.

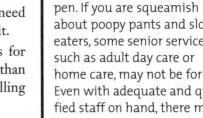

Beware!
Accept the reality that accidents happen. If you are squeamish about poopy pants and sloppy eaters, some senior services, such as adult day care or home care, may not be for you. Even with adequate and qualified staff on hand, there may be times when you will be required to take care of some of your clients' more intimate needs.

Experience Is the Best Teacher

Often, the best way to learn more about yourself and others is to become personally involved in the daily operations of a business similar to the one you want to start. Get a job working with a company providing the services you intend to offer. You'll gain important experience in the realities and logistics of the operation that will give you a solid foundation for your own business.

When doing your market research, take classes or join organizations and volunteer groups that are committed to elder care. Allen Hager, owner and founder of Omaha, Nebraska-based Right at Home, took this idea a step further by becoming a certified nursing assistant and working as an aide for about eight months. "I had always been on the desk side of health care, and I knew that I would never have another opportunity to do this," he says. After taking the 75-hour course, passing the test, and becoming certified, Hager worked 12-hour shifts on weekends at a local nursing home. This experience gave him insight into senior citizens and the issues that concern them.

- *Compassion.* You need to be able to demonstrate understanding and encouragement with seniors whose capacities are failing.
- *Knowledge.* You can be a tremendous asset to your elderly clients by having information about various services available to senior citizens, both locally and nationwide.

The Daily Grind

Your daily operations will vary substantially based on the senior services business you start. You must understand what you need to do in the way of administration and operations, and set up systems from the beginning that allow you to efficiently deal with the issues you'll encounter on a daily basis.

Keep in mind that you don't have to do everything yourself, even if you decide you want to be a one-person show. You can outsource some of your administrative functions, such as billing. You can hire someone to design your website. You can take advantage of convenience services offered by suppliers to make your purchasing and inventory management easier.

In the next chapter, we'll discuss creating a business plan that will get you started on the right foot.

3

Developing
Your Plan

Regardless of how well you think you know your business, you need a written business plan. Writing your plans down forces you to think them through and gives you a chance to examine them for consistency and thoroughness.

Some entrepreneurs would rather walk on hot coals than sit down and write a business plan. Other would-be business owners get so caught up in planning every detail that they never get their business off the ground. You need to find a happy medium between these two extremes.

This chapter will focus on a few issues particular to planning a business serving the senior market, but they are by no means all you need to consider when writing your plan.

Enjoy the Process

If you're excited about your business, creating a business plan should be an exciting process. It will help you define and evaluate the overall feasibility of your concept, clarify your goals, and determine what you'll need for startup and long-term operations.

This is a living, breathing document that will provide you with a road map for your company. You'll use it as a guide, referring to it regularly as you work through the startup process and then during the operation of your business. And if you're going to be seeking outside financing, either in the form of loans or investors, your business plan will be the tool that convinces funding sources of the worthiness of your venture.

Putting together a business plan is not a linear process, although the final product may look that way. As you work through it, you'll likely find yourself jumping from defining your service package to cash flow forecasts to staffing, then back to cash flow, on to marketing, and back to your service package. Take your time developing your plan; whether you want to start a one-person concierge service or a chain of home health-care operations, you're making a serious commitment, and you shouldn't rush it.

Beware!
When you make a change to one part of your business plan, be sure you think through how that change will affect the rest of your operation. For example, if you start out offering in-home concierge services and later decide to add shopping and errand-running, will this change your equipment needs (in particular, your vehicle)?

Choosing Your Niche

Before you can begin any serious business planning, you must first decide what part of the senior services industry you want to enter. We will talk specifically in later chapters about senior day care, relocation services, home care and home health-care, concierge services, transportation services, and travel services for seniors. As you consider the niche you want to serve, think about your own likes and dislikes, skills, and resources. For example, if you don't like dealing with sick people, then home health care is definitely not for you. If you like a variety of activities and would prefer not to be tied to an office, a concierge service could be for you.

Dick Padgett of San Diego's Five Star Concierge stumbled into his business by accident. He had been out of work for quite some time and was taking care of his wife's grandmother by providing transportation to the doctor's office and taking her on shopping expeditions when he realized that there was a serious need for that type of service in his area. From there, his business quickly expanded to include other types of concierge services, including errand-running and handyman services.

Before starting Right at Home in Omaha, Nebraska, Allen Hager was vice president of corporate development for a large health-care company. In that job, he analyzed the senior market and its impact on the health industry. His findings raised his own concerns about seniors who do not need institutional care but who can't quite manage on their own, so he decided to jump into the home health-care business.

Once you have decided on the best niche for you, determine if there is a market for your business.

Whom Will You Serve?

The first step is to identify your customers. Draw a picture of who your typical client is, considering issues such as gender, age, physical and mental disabilities, and income. Think about senior preferences as they relate to your business. Will you need comfortable chairs, a television and magazines, or coffee in the waiting area? Will you have potential customers who may have physical limitations that require the use of handrails or ramps at entryways?

If your clients are likely to suffer from dementia or other handicaps and the decision to use your services will probably be made by someone else, think about who that person might be. Again, draw a picture of the caregiver—is this person an adult child, a sibling, another relative, an attorney? These visuals are important because you want to view your business through their eyes. Being able to relate to clients and their specific needs is the way that successful entrepreneurs operate.

Perhaps your clients are retirees who want to enjoy life to its fullest by traveling and making new friends. Then you may envision a financially secure senior who has the potential to become a customer for many years using your customized travel services.

When you know what you want to do and whom you want to serve, you can do the market research necessary to determine the viability of your business.

Researching Your Market

Tip...

Smart Tip

Keep geography in mind •
as you define your market. For
many seniors, transportation
is an issue. You want your
business to be easily accessible to clients, or vice versa, if
you are traveling to them.

An in-depth examination of your market is essential to your success. Market research provides you with data that helps you identify and reach particular market segments and to solve or avoid marketing problems. A thorough market survey forms the foundation of any successful business. It would be impossible to develop marketing strategies or an effective product or service line without market research.

Decide on the geographic area you want to serve, and determine if there are enough people in that area who meet your customer profile. You may, for example, want to establish an upscale adult day-care center, but your research tells you that there are not enough potential clients in the geographic area you've defined who can afford your rates. In that case, you have two choices: You can either change the geographic area or you can change your strategy to target middle- and lower-income clients.

What is wrong with just going after anybody in the world who might ever need adult day care for any reason? Because that market segment includes literally millions of people, and it's impossible for any small business to communicate effectively with that many people. Can you afford to send even one piece of direct mail to one million prospective customers? Of course not. But when you narrow that market down to 500 or 1,000 prospective clients in a particular area, launching a successful direct-mail campaign is affordable and manageable.

There are additional reasons for choosing a well-defined market niche. By targeting a very specific market segment, you can tailor your service package and marketing efforts to meet that audience's needs. This focus helps you be more productive and ultimately more profitable. In addition, you can position yourself as an expert in your niche, which is a marketing advantage.

Market research also gives you information about your competitors. You need to find out what they're doing and how that meets your market's needs.

Bright Idea

As the internet increases in popularity, you'll find most of your competitors have websites, which you can visit to find out what type of services they offer. Or you can simply call them, pretending to be a prospective customer, and ask about what they do, how they operate, and how much they charge.

A key competitive issue many senior service businesses need to consider is that your competition will often be nonprofit public or private agencies that may charge significantly less than you will. If this is the case, address it in your business plan by discussing how you will compete on service.

One of the most basic elements of effective marketing is differentiating yourself from the competition. One marketing consultant calls it "eliminating the competition," because if you set yourself apart by doing something no one else does, then you essentially have no competition. However, before you can differentiate yourself, you need to understand who your competitors are and why your customers might patronize them. Offering something no one else does could give you an edge in the market—but it could also mean that someone else has tried that avenue and it didn't work. Don't make hasty decisions; do your homework before finalizing your services.

Are You on a Mission?

At any given moment, most senior services business owners have a clear understanding of their company's missions. They know what they are doing, how and where it's being done, and who their customers are. Problems can arise, however, when that mission is not clearly articulated into a statement, written down, and communicated to others.

Even in a very small company, a written mission statement helps everyone involved see the big picture and keeps them focused on the business's goals. At a minimum, your mission statement should define who your primary customers are, identify your products and services, and perhaps describe the geographical location in which you operate. A mission statement should be short—usually just one sentence and certainly no more than two. For example, Hager's mission statement concisely states: "The Mission of Right at Home is to improve the quality of life for those we serve." A good idea is to cap it at 100 words. Anything longer than that isn't a mission statement and will probably confuse your employees. Use the Mission Statement Worksheet on page 21 to help write yours.

Once you've articulated your message, communicate it as often as possible to everyone in the company, along with customers and suppliers. Post it on the wall, hold meetings to talk about it, and include a reminder of the statement in all employee correspondence.

It's more important to adequately communicate the mission statement to employees than to customers. Sometimes companies try to use their mission statements for promotion, then as an aside use it to help their employees understand the business. That doesn't work very well. The most effective mission statements are developed strictly for internal communication and discussion, and then if something

▲

Mission Statement Worksheet

To develop an effective mission statement, answer these questions:

1. What products and/or services do we offer? _____

   _____

2. What geographical location do we operate in? _____

   _____

3. Why does my company exist? Whom do we serve? What is our purpose?

   _____

   _____

4. What are our strengths, weaknesses, opportunities, and threats? _____

   _____

5. Considering the above, along with our expertise and resources, what business should we be in?_____

   _____

6. What is important to us? What do we stand for? _____

   _____

Using this information, write your mission statement here:

Mission statement for: _____

(your business's name)

_____

_____

_____

_____

_____

promotional comes out of it, great. In other words, your mission statement doesn't have to be clever or catchy—just accurate.

Although your mission statement may never win an advertising or creativity award, it can still be a very effective customer relations tool. One idea is to print your mission statement on a poster-sized panel, have every employee sign it, and hang it in a prominent place so clients can see it. You can even include it on your brochures and invoices. Karen Martin, an antiques hobbyist turned entrepreneur of a moving management firm in Hartford, Connecticut, prominently displays her mission statement on all of her brochures and on her website which reads: "Downsizing a home is a special passage in life—one that deserves time, caring attention and practical support."

> **Bright Idea**
> Update your business plan every year. Choose an annual date when you sit down with your plan, compare how closely your actual operation and results followed your forecasts, and decide if your plans for the coming year need adjusting. You will also need to take your financial forecasts out for another year, based on current and expected market conditions.

Finally, make sure your suppliers know what your mission statement is; it will help them serve you better if they understand what you're all about.

Time to Write the Plan

Once you've identified the products and services you want to offer and to whom, and have created your mission statement, you're ready to complete your business plan.

Though the content of your business plan will be unique, there is a basic format that you should follow. This will ensure that you address all the necessary issues, as well as provide lenders and investors with a document organized in a familiar way to evaluate.

- *Cover sheet.* Add your business name, address, phone number, fax number, email address, and website.
- *Table of contents.* A TOC can be used as a working outline; be sure to add page numbers.
- *Executive summary.* This provides a brief synopsis of your senior services business.
- *Mission statement.* Describe your vision, values, services, and philosophy.
- *Marketing plan.* Provides an overview of the market and identifies the competition.
- *Organizational plan.* Identify your legal structure, and provide short-term objectives and long-range goals.

- *Management plan*. Discuss how you plan to manage your business and what your qualifications are.
- *Financial plan*. Identify startup capital and financial projections.
- *Summary*. Bring your plan together in this section.
- *Appendices*. Include supporting documents such as resumes, permits, leases, and references.

When you think your business plan is complete, look at it with a fresh eye. Is it a true and honest representation of the facts? Is it realistic? Does it consider all the possible variables that could affect your operation? After you're satisfied, show the plan to two or three professional associates whose input you value and trust. Ask them to be brutally honest with their evaluations; you need to know if there are any glaring problems with your plan so you can correct them before they cost you time and money.

Now let's take a look at what's involved in starting and running a senior day-care business.

4

Adult Day-Care
Service

oday's baby boomers face a dual challenge:

They're caring for their own children, and sometimes grandchil-

dren, as well as caring for their parents. Middle-aged people

who are trying to balance providing appropriate care for aging

parents and their own youngsters are known as the sandwich

generation, and many of them desperately need the break a

senior adult day-care center provides. The burden of caring for older family members can be overwhelming, and a place where these seniors can socialize and participate in activities in a safe, supervised environment is a welcome option for their stressed care-givers.

Adult day-care centers range from small, individually owned operations that offer all the comforts of a close-knit family home to commercially based businesses that include a wide range of services. Some are structured to meet the needs of functional seniors who don't need special care; others are designed for cognitively impaired and/or chronically ill senior clients. And some provide a safe, nurturing environment for clients in all categories.

Senior adult day-care centers bridge the gap between home care by a family care-giver and institutional care in a nursing facility. Elderly people who have suffered strokes, are in rehabilitation from surgery or an injury, have memory loss or demen-tia, physical disabilities or limitations, or visual problems are potential clients for a senior adult day-care center. There are two types of senior adult day-care centers: social and medical. Currently, informal social centers are more prevalent. They usu-ally cater to seniors who have a higher level of functioning, although many clients may be wheelchair-bound, incontinent, or need limited assistance with daily activities. The focus in this type of setting is more on activities, social interaction, and meals. A medical day-care center provides a more complex level of care and has a registered nurse on staff who can perform tube feedings, administer medications and oxygen, and pro-vide other related care.

Stat Fact

According to the National Adult Day Services Association, the average age of the adult day-care consumer is 72, and two-thirds of all participants are women. Fifty-nine percent of the participants require assis-tance with two or more activi-ties of daily living: eating, bathing, dressing, toileting, or transferring; 41 percent require assistance in three or more areas.

Typically, these programs operate during the same standard business hours of a tradi-tional child day-care center, which is usually 8 A.M. to 6 P.M. Some clients may attend a senior adult day-care program a few hours a week, while others visit every day. Many centers offer respite services in the evenings and/or on week-ends.

The demand for adult day care is outpacing the supply. According to a national survey by MetLife Mature Market Institute, there are approximately 4,600 centers operating in the United States, assisting more than 150,000 Americans each day. But many more are needed—and as America ages, that need will increase.

Not All Day-Care Centers Are the Same

Senior adult day-care centers typically offer a wide variety of services, and you can put together a combination that ranges from simple to complex. Some day-care centers only provide a social outlet for seniors a few hours a day, while others offer a greater range of services, including caring for seniors with specific conditions, such as memory loss or dementia, limited mobility, or incontinence.

Depending on your goals and resources, you can start out small and stay small, earning a comfortable income; you can start out small and grow; or you can start by opening a substantial enterprise with a wide range of services and full staff. A good approach is to start by providing a relatively small number of services, then expand in both your offerings and your capacity as your business becomes established and you learn exactly what your clients and their families want and need.

Services you may provide include:

- Recreational and social activities
- Exercise, including chair aerobics
- Hot meals and nutritious snacks
- Respite care (weekends or nights)
- Extended hours
- Transportation
- Escorts for medical appointments
- Assistance with eating, walking, toileting, and medicines
- Personal care (bathing, shaving, grooming, dressing, foot care)
- Rehabilitation therapy
- Counseling
- Social services
- Nursing services
- Health monitoring (check blood pressure, temperature, and insulin levels)
- Support groups and educational seminars for clients, caregivers, and the community

> **Tip...**
>
> **Smart Tip**
>
> The National Adult Day Services Association (NASDA) offers a vast selection of publications and resources for adult day services including standards and guidelines, marketing strategies, surveys, and training resources for employees. Visit nadsa.org or call (877) 745-1440 for more information.

Activities and Programs

Senior adult day-care centers are not glorified babysitting services where you turn the TV channel to a game show or soap opera while keeping a watchful eye on Gramps to make sure he doesn't wander off. You need to offer programs that entertain, enrich, and inspire your senior charges. These recreational activities can be in the form of arts and crafts, exercise groups, pet therapy, games, and music therapy. Like everyone, older people like to feel useful; doing volunteer work, such as stuffing envelopes for a church or community organization, is a task even your wheelchair-bound clients can handle and enjoy.

> **Bright Idea**
>
> Make your clients' birthdays a celebration. The parties are always fun, and seniors enjoy the special attention. Purchase inexpensive party hats and favors, and announce the event ahead of time. Keep your clients' dietary requirements in mind, and make sure the refreshments include treats everyone can enjoy.

Most older folks thrive on routine, so it will be important to have a predictable schedule. A typical day might look like this: personal grooming at 8 A.M., snacks at 9:30 A.M., special activity at 10 A.M., lunch at 11:45 A.M., quiet time with a movie at 1:30 P.M., snacks at 3 P.M., followed by a group discussion or another activity at 3:30 P.M. It's important to provide a variety of structured activities for individuals and groups that are designed to stimulate and entertain your senior clients during the day. You may want to hire a program director to plan and organize activities.

Unlike participating at a senior community center, where they often go on field trips, your clients will remain at your facility, and you will bring the field trips to them in the form of guest speakers and live entertainment. Get the word out and invite the drama club from a neighboring school, a choir from a local church, or a safety presentation from a Scout group. Your seniors may also appreciate a demonstration by the local fire or police department.

Meal Preparation

Most adult day-care centers offer nutritious snacks and hot meals as part of their programs. When preparing menus, be aware that many of your clients will have special dietary needs you'll have to accommodate.

On-premises meal preparation means you'll need a commercial kitchen that meets the requirements of your local health department. Expect the kitchen to take up about 15 to 20 percent of your total space. Within this area, you will need space for receiving, storage, food preparation, cooking, cleanup, and trash storage. You will also need room for a large refrigerator/freezer and a pantry or wall shelves for dry food storage.

An alternative to on-site meal preparation is to use a catering service. You may find this more efficient and reliable than trying to prepare meals yourself or hiring a cook, and the difference in overall cost may not be significant. Diane Ross, owner and founder of Reno, Nevada's The Continuum, which features an adult day-care center, decided it would be cost-prohibitive to have a commercial kitchen with an on-site cooking staff, so she has all hot meals catered.

> ### Bright Idea
> Prepare a monthly calendar with your meal menu, and make it available to your clients and their caregivers. Your clients can arrange for alternative meals and snacks on the days you're serving something they don't want to eat.

Transportation

In most cases, getting to and from your center is the responsibility of the clients or their caregivers. You may choose to offer limited transportation services, such as taking clients to medical appointments or on other errands during the day. Of course, adding transportation to your service package means investing in vehicles, insuring them, and hiring drivers—but it can be lucrative. See Chapter 8 for more on starting a senior transportation service.

Another transportation option is to contract with an established transportation company that provides the level of service your clients need. You can pay the transportation company and bill the fees back to your clients (with a markup, of course) or just refer your clients to the company and stay out of the transaction. Because the safety and security of your clients and your own reputation are at stake, thoroughly check out any transportation company you use or recommend. Ask for proof of insurance, find out how their drivers are screened and trained, be sure they have the type of vehicles and equipment your clients need, and check their references. It's also a good idea to check with the Better Business Bureau and your state's Attorney General's office to see if any complaints have been filed.

Getting Started

Depending on what type of program you are starting—social or medical—and how many seniors you anticipate serving, startup costs could be as low as $10,000, or as much as $250,000. Unless you are homebased, your facility will likely be your biggest expense. Consider: How many seniors do you want to serve? Do you want to have a commercial kitchen or medical facilities? Will you rent your space or buy it?

A Better Pill to Swallow

Most of your senior clients will need to take medication daily. If you do not have a licensed health-care worker on staff to administer these, make it your policy that your clients need to be able to take the medicine themselves. Of course, they will be closely monitored and supervised by your staff.

Staff members should know the clients to whom they are administering medication. If they don't, they should ask another staff member to verify the client's identity before providing any drugs. Whether prescription or nonprescription, keep all drugs clearly marked and stored in a safe place. Any narcotics should be kept in a locked cabinet. Use a separate refrigerator to store drugs requiring refrigeration.

Prescription drugs should be in the original container or package, clearly marked with the patient's name, drug name, and dosage instructions; prescription date and expiration date; and name and phone number of the doctor or other prescribing health professional.

Nonprescribed, over-the-counter medication should be treated with the same respect by clearly labeling the package with the patient's name, dosage instructions, expiration date, and the contact information of the doctor or health professional who recommended the medicine.

Because health circumstances requiring medication are diverse, some clients may want to take medication on an "as-needed" basis, and you will need to set a policy on how to deal with this issue. For instance, a senior client may need emergency oxygen, glucagon for low blood sugar, have an allergic reaction that requires an epinephrine injection, or want an analgesic for an upset stomach. Some day-care providers do not administer medications "as needed," but others may do so. Check with your attorney to make sure you have the appropriate releases on file if you decide you will provide this service. Then set a policy wherein the staff member administering the medication documents the dosage in writing on the medication log and in a note or on a form to be sent home to the caregiver so they will know when and why medication was given.

Use the Prescription Medication Permission Form and Medication Log on pages 30 and 31 to manage your clients' medications.

Whether you start a homebased or commercially based operation, it should have adequate, open space. Some adult day-care centers use storefront properties in shopping centers and strip malls. These can be quickly and efficiently turned into practical setups with the use of dividers and partitions that provide necessary room definition while still making it easy for wheelchairs and walkers to move around. Vinyl or tile

Day-Care Center Equipment Checklist

☐ 4 recliners	$1,000–$5,000
☐ 4 armchairs	$700–$3,200
☐ 1 couch/sofa	$500–$4,000
☐ 2 standard wheelchairs	$300–$600
☐ 2 standard walkers	$150–$500
☐ 2 LCD or LED TVs	$600–$4,000
☐ 2 DVD or Blu-ray players	$70–$600
☐ 10 DVD or Blu-ray movies	$100–$250
☐ 1 CD player/stereo/radio	$50–$500
☐ 1-year subscription to 2 to 3 consumer magazines	$15–$60
☐ 1 local newspaper subscription	$75–$125
☐ 4 board games	$40–$100
☐ 4 decks of cards	$6–$10
☐ 10 cubicles for storage	$40–$150
☐ 20 books (hardcover)	$200–$400
☐ 20 bath towels	$70–$400
☐ 20 hand towels	$40–$300
☐ 20 washcloths	$20–$100
☐ 1 case disposable underwear	$50–$75
☐ First-aid kit	$15–$150

Prescription Medication Permission Form

Client's name: _____

Caregiver/legal guardian: _____

Address: _____

Phone: _____ Email: _____

Physician: _____

Address: _____

Phone: _____

Medication: _____

Dosage: _____

Time of day: _____

Reason for medication: _____

Possible side effects: _____

Special instructions (refrigeration needed, special equipment, or apparatus required, crush in food, ointment applied to skin, drops in eyes, etc.): _____

_____

_____

Procedures: All medications (including over-the-counter) must be in the original container with client's full name, dosage instructions, and expiration date clearly marked, along with the name and phone number of the prescribing licensed health professional.

I hereby give permission to _____ (name of senior adult day-care center) to administer the above-referenced medication(s) to _____ (name of senior person) as instructed on this form.

Caregiver/legal guardian: _____
                                              signature

Date: _____

Verified by: (director) _____
                                              signature

Date: _____

Medication Log

Client's name: _____

Prescription Medication Permission Form(s) signed and dated:

    Yes _____ No _____

(Attach authorization forms to this log)

Date: _____ Time: _____

Medication: _____

Dosage: _____

Given by: _____

Comments: _____

_____

_____

_____

_____

_____

_____

_____

flooring is preferred over carpet, which can impede maneuverability. Your facility needs to be completely handicapped-accessible to meet the needs of your clients as well as the law. Ross says The Continuum's space is very open, with a library area furnished with recliners and a TV. The dining room area is designed for a variety of activities in addition to meals.

Other essentials you will need include recliners, sofas, chairs with arms, at least one spare wheelchair and an extra walker, one or more televisions with DVD players, books, cards and board games, and a storage area for clients' personal items. Beds are generally not needed for your day-care clients; if they want to snooze, they can use the recliners or a couch. See the itemized equipment list for suggestions and estimated prices to help set up your senior adult day-care center.

How Much Should You Charge?

Daily fees for adult day care range from $40 to $75 per day, with the average around $61. Unlike nonprofit centers, which often charge on a sliding scale, your center should offer the same rates to everyone based on the services they use. Rates are typically lower for a social adult day-care center than a medical adult day-care center because fewer services are provided and licensed medical staff is not required.

To determine your fees, do a survey of what centers providing similar services in your area are charging. Calculate your operational costs and figure out how much revenue per hour per client you need to cover your expenses and allow for a profit.

Start by walking through the process of figuring out what it costs you per hour to operate. Include the rent, utilities, overhead, staffing, and profit, divided by the total hours you are open. This will tell you what your expenses and profit are per hour. If your staffing level allows you to care for X number of clients, then you need to charge your total expenses and profit divided by that number of clients.

> **Tip...**
>
> **Smart Tip**
> Suggest that caregivers ask their pharmacists to divide prescribed medication into two containers—one for home use and one to be kept at the day-care center.

For example: If you determine your expenses are $200 per hour and you want a profit of 30 percent, your total would be $260 per hour. Then if your staff can handle six clients at a time, you would charge $260 divided by six, for a fee of $43 per hour per client.

Finally, consider your target market and what they can afford. Ideally, those three numbers will be very close, and you can set your fees based on that. If they're not—if, for example, based on your costs you need to charge one and a half times the going rate in your market to break even—then you need to go back to your plan and figure out where you can adjust.

Licenses and Certifications

Adult day-care centers fall under the jurisdiction of various state and local government entities. Contact your state's Department of Social Services or Department of Health to find out what licenses and certifications are necessary, and what other requirements you must meet. Also check with your county health department, the local fire department, and your county or city business licensing agency to make sure you are in full compliance with all applicable laws.

Be Prepared!

Many injuries are not life-threatening and don't require immediate medical attention. However, knowing how to treat minor injuries is a necessity when operating an adult day-care center. In addition to taking a first-aid class, Ready America (ready.gov) recommends having the following first-aid supplies on hand in the event of an emergency:

Things you should have:

- ○ Two pairs of Latex, or other sterile gloves (if you are allergic to Latex)
- ○ Sterile dressings to stop bleeding
- ○ Cleansing agent/soap and antibiotic towelettes to disinfect
- ○ Antibiotic ointment to prevent infection
- ○ Burn ointment to prevent infection
- ○ Adhesive bandages in a variety of sizes
- ○ Eye wash solution to flush the eyes or as general decontaminant
- ○ Thermometer

Things it may be good to have:

- ○ Cell phone
- ○ Scissors
- ○ Tweezers
- ○ Tube of petroleum jelly or other lubricant

Non-prescription drugs:

- ○ Aspirin or nonaspirin pain reliever
- ○ Anti-diarrhea medication
- ○ Antacid (for upset stomach)
- ○ Laxative

If your center is appropriately licensed, certified, or accredited, your clients may be eligible to receive financial benefits from the government. For example, under Public Law 106–117 of the Veteran's Millennium Health Care & Benefits Act, eligible veterans can receive funds for noninstitutional extended-care services, such as those services provided by an adult day-care center. For more information, contact the Department of Veterans Affairs (see the Appendix for contact details).

Also, the National Family Caregiver Support Program (Title III of the Older Americans Act) has a broad array of support services. Although funds are limited, they can sometimes provide financial relief to caregivers in need of respite care. They can be contacted through the U.S. Administration on Aging (see Appendix for contact information).

> ### Bright Idea
> Every few months, send home a survey to clients' families to see what specific services they would find the most useful, and then see how you can implement those to keep your clients happy.

In some states, Medicaid reimbursements or other state-funded health insurance programs (e.g., Medi-Cal in California) are available for eligible participants in qualified, licensed adult day-care centers. Private insurance companies will sometimes pay for senior adult day-care if it is determined that the elderly person would otherwise need to go to a nursing home. Also, IRS tax credits may be available for using an adult day-care center when caring for an elderly family member.

Medicare funds are not currently available to cover adult day-care costs, but Congress is always tinkering with Medicare benefits, so pay attention to legislation that might benefit your center or your clients.

Even though some private insurance and government financial assistance may be available, most of your clients will pay for your services out of their own pockets. You may even prefer that they do if you don't want to haggle with all the stipulations and requirements that might otherwise be imposed on your center by federal, state, and local authorities.

Most of the clients at The Continuum pay with private funds; however, because the center is licensed and accredited, it has a contract with the state of Nevada that allows it to provide services for eligible seniors. Ross says the center also accepts clients who have respite grant funding.

Put It in Writing

Your contract should clearly outline the services you provide, the costs of those services, and terms of payment. It should be signed by you and either your client or the person responsible for your client, and copies should be provided to both parties.

Policies and Procedures

It's important to think through your policies completely before you open for business. Give each client or caregiver a copy of your policies as part of his or her contract, and have an acknowledgment signed that the client has read, understood, and agreed to abide by your rules. Your policy statement should address such issues as:

- *Hours of operation*, including days of the week and holiday closings.
- *Fee structure*, including rates, when payments are due, late payment policies, and any circumstances under which you expect to be paid even though your client wasn't there.
- *What sort of notice is required* when clients deviate from their expected schedule.
- *Whether you allow unexpected drop-ins.*
- *Whether you will accept clients who are ill.* A common policy is for day-care centers to insist that clients with contagious conditions such as colds or the flu stay home until they are well so they do not infect your other clients.
- *How you will deal with clients who exhibit aggressive or violent behavior, or who have chronic adjustment issues.* Most day-care facilities are not equipped to care for someone who poses a danger to himself or others.
- *Your plan for weather or other natural disasters.* For example, your policy may be that if local public schools are closed due to snow, hurricane, or other threatening conditions, you will also be closed.
- *Holiday schedule.* List the holidays on which you will close, and whether you expect to be paid for those days.
- *Vacation schedule.* If you are a homebased solo operator, your clients need to know well in advance when you will be closed for your own vacation.

Go over your contracts and policies annually and make sure they are still meeting your needs. If you make changes, provide copies of the new information to your clients and their caregivers. Have them sign and date a statement or addendum acknowledging that they have received a copy of the revisions, have read and understand them, and agree to abide by them.

Hours of Operation

Naturally your fees and hours of operation will be dictated by the type of services you offer. By opening your center during nontraditional hours—early mornings, evenings and weekends—you can broaden your market and increase revenue. Some day-care centers offer respite care for just a few hours a day—for example, 10 A.M. to

4 P.M. Others operate on a typical business-day schedule of 8 A.M. to 5 P.M. Still others offer extended hours either every day or on certain days. Consider your market and your own staffing resources when setting your hours.

Seasonal Issues

Adult day cares experience some seasonal fluctuations. You may see a drop-off in business during the winter holidays and perhaps over the

> **Bright Idea**
> Have a locker, basket, or box designated for each senior who comes to your center that will hold items such as extra clothing, disposable underwear, books, games, and other personal items.

summer, when many families go on vacation. As part of your policies, you will want to specify whether you will require advance notice when a client is not going to be there. With enough notice, you may be able to temporarily fill the gap with another client and not lose any revenue on those days. If you are expected to reserve a space in your program during a client's absence, you will need to decide if you will charge them the full rate, a discounted rate, or no fees at all.

Safety, Emergency, and Reporting Policies

Safety is an integral part of everything you do in the operation of your senior adult day-care center. Incorporate the following health and safety issues into your policies and procedures:

- *Admission and discharge*. Establish a procedure to sign clients in and out on their arrival and departure each day. This is an important safety measure in the event some of your clients have a tendency to wander off, or to prevent their leaving with an unauthorized person. You will need to maintain daily attendance records even if your center has clients who admit themselves or does not have a "locked door" policy, allowing seniors to come and go at will.

- *Inspections*. All licensed day-care centers are subject to inspection by various state and local authorities, including the health department. When any deficiencies are identified during an inspection or review by a licensing agency, funding agency, accreditation organization, or other regulatory department, develop a written plan for the resolution. The plan should include a description of the problem, proposed timeline for the resolution, designation of responsibility for correcting the deficiency, and a description of the successful resolution of the problem.

- *Fire safety*. Fire extinguishers should be inspected every three months, and smoke alarms should have their batteries replaced every six months. Regular evacuation drills should be held, and records of such events, along with safety maintenance logs, should be kept on file.

▲

Between You and Me . . .

It's important that clients or family members disclose pertinent health information about the people in your care; however, you should not release this information to anyone else without the written consent of the client or caregiver.

Under federal guidelines for the Health Insurance Portability and Accountability Act of 1996 (HIPAA), adult day-care centers must establish procedures that will safeguard the confidentiality of their clients' medical records. Set up policies and closely monitor how information is shared internally and externally. This includes training your staff and volunteers, installing appropriate computer software, monitoring passwords, keeping paper records in locked cabinets, and taking other steps to protect these sensitive files.

For more information and detailed guidelines on how to implement HIPAA rules, check out the U.S. Department of Health and Human Services website at dhhs.gov/ocr/hipaa.

- *Health department reporting requirements.* Certain diseases or conditions among your clients or your staff must be reported to the local health department. Some examples are communicable diseases such as chicken pox, measles, and hepatitis. For more information on reporting requirements and procedures, contact your local health department.
- *Emergencies.* You should have written procedures that your staff is expected to follow in the event of an accident, injury, sickness, or emergency evacuation. Emergency phone numbers for doctors and caregivers should be immediately accessible.
- *Elder abuse.* If you suspect that one of your clients is being abused—whether it is physically, emotionally, or financially—you must report it to your local department of protective services or equivalent agency.
- *Client records.* Maintain detailed and up-to-date records on your clients, including consent forms, medical information, attendance records, and incident reports. Keep a separate file for each client in a secure location.
- *Confidentiality.* Establish policies and procedures covering the exchange of information among clients, caregivers, staff, and other professionals or agencies that are involved with your clients. Your policies should address information obtained before the clients enter your facility's care, during the time you are caring for them, and after they leave.

▲

Staffing

Generally, the employees at an adult day-care center should be people who enjoy working with seniors, have tremendous patience, and are flexible enough to deal with various personalities and administrative tasks. You may be able to start with just yourself and perhaps one other care provider, but eventually you may need a receptionist, a bookkeeper, possibly a driver, a cook (or meal coordinator), and more care providers.

How you will handle staffing your company should be addressed in detail in your business plan. The mechanics of staffing—including finding, screening, and hiring employees; benefits; salary ranges; and other personnel issues—are discussed in Chapter 12.

There are many similarities between adult day care and child day care in terms of contracts, equipment, hours, licensing, staffing, and management. Therefore, you may find it helpful to read Entrepreneur's *Start Your Own Child-Care Business*.

Relocation
Service

Many people in the rapidly growing 70-and-over population segment are selling their homes in favor of smaller houses or condos, either in traditional neighborhoods or retirement communities. This is a perfect time to cater to the relocation needs of this market.

Moving is always stressful, and it can be especially traumatic for someone who is leaving a home he or she has been in for decades that is full of precious memories. Adding to the challenge is the fact that families are more spread out geographically and not always available to help with the moving process, which can be a tremendous burden for seniors. Not only is the packing and cleaning process physically demanding; it also takes an emotional toll. A senior relocation consultant can provide an element of compassionate objectivity as decisions are made about what to keep, give away, sell, or toss.

Karen Martin, owner and founder of Life Moves, LLC, a moving management firm in Hartford, Connecticut, started her company in 1998 to help people make successful mid- and later-life moves. "I guide families in gaining meaning and comfort from the process of sorting through their treasures," she says. She provides a variety of services to assist in downsizing or emptying a home and getting it ready for market or closing.

As a senior relocation specialist, you can offer a wide range of services. It's typical to provide a total turnkey package, which means you'll orchestrate every aspect of the move, including:

- Assistance with selling the current home
- Assistance with finding a new residence
- Assistance with selecting a moving company
- Sorting and downsizing
- Estate sales
- Coordinating movers, utilities, cleaning, and other tasks
- Packing and unpacking

Of course, no two moves will be alike, because each of your clients and situations will be unique. Martin's services include sorting through everything in the house: garage, basement, attic, garden shed, and outer buildings. "I assist in the selection of furnishings and other possessions that the clients might want for their new home if they need that help," she says. "I have offered packing, unpacking, and setting up their new homes. I also coordinate onsite estate sales of leftover furnishings, or I may arrange for other methods of liquidation—either buying out or auctioning." She will also take care of shredding old financial and personal documents, donating, recycling, and refuse removal.

Stat Fact

Approximately 41 percent of sellers in the real estate market are people over the age of 55. With baby boomers now entering retirement, this market is quickly expanding. A Senior Real Estate Specialist (SRES) is a designation for real estate agents who want to specialize in this niche.

Senior relocation specialists typically do not operate moving and storage companies; rather, they contract with those companies, as well as common carrier and small-package carriers, depending on clients' needs. Starting a trucking company is a capital- and equipment-intensive operation that goes beyond the scope of this guide. But existing carriers will be happy to work with you to service your clients.

Senior relocation specialists also enlist the help of independent contractors and professionals, such as real estate agents, appraisers, cleaning services, and concierge services, which broaden the scope of their services to meet the various needs of their clients.

Coordinating the Move

Even though many household moving companies bill themselves as "relocation specialists," they do not target the senior market with the same degree of personal attention and compassion that you will.

The most common service a senior relocation specialist provides falls under the umbrella of coordinating the move. It's your job to make sure everything gets handled and nothing gets overlooked. Although the specific service package you offer each client will vary depending on individual needs, be prepared to offer the following.

Health-Related Services

If the client is moving to a new hometown, they will need to find a new physician, hospital, dentist, and pharmacy. His or her current doctor and pharmacist can make recommendations, but this should be done prior to the move in the event your client needs medical attention immediately following the move. Most medical offices have their own medical records transfer request forms, so make sure the appropriate paperwork and insurance information are forwarded to the correct offices in a timely manner.

Utilities

Schedule connect and disconnect dates with all the utility companies: gas, water, sewer, electricity, telephone, cable, sanitation, etc. Usually utilities are turned on at the new residence the day before the move and turned off at the old dwelling the day after the move. Give a detailed list to clients with scheduled termination and activation dates for their review and approval.

▲

Some utility companies will not allow a third party to place service orders without written permission from the account holder. In that event, you'll need to have a notarized letter of authorization from your client. See the Letter of Authorization for Utility Company on page 43.

Notifications

Help your client put together a list of everyone who needs an address-change notification, and then handle that administrative task. Pick up a change-of-address kit from any U.S. Post Office (or go online to moversguide.usps.com) to assist with this process. Use the cards the post office provides for notifying magazines and newspapers, and for filing a change-of-address notice. For credit card companies, financial service companies and other service providers, help your client use the change-of-address form on his or her monthly statement. Or check for toll-free numbers to save time and postage.

You can add a special personal touch to your services by sending attractive change-of-address cards to the client's family and friends. Such cards are available in any retail store that sells greeting cards, or you can create your own.

Assist your clients with notifying their financial institutions of the pending move, which may also include asking the bank to arrange the transfer of the contents of a safe deposit box to another branch or bank in the new hometown. If the client has direct deposit or automatic payments set up, these will also need to be transferred or discontinued. Also, the client's insurance agent will need to be notified to cancel or transfer homeowner's coverage.

If the client belongs to any clubs or associations, determine if he will need to sell, transfer, refund or resign the memberships.

Travel Arrangements

You may need to help your clients with their travel—especially if they're moving to another city. This job can be made easier by using the services of a senior travel agent who understands and can meet any special needs your clients may have. See Chapter 9 for complete details on senior travel services.

If they plan to drive a long distance, arrange to have their car serviced before they hit the road. Or if they're disabled or infirm, you can make arrangements to provide chauffeur service or an attendant on moving day. Meal service can be provided as well.

Bright Idea

If your clients are traveling by automobile, pack a "trip kit" of necessary items for them to take in their car. Include bottled water, snacks, paper towels, wet wipes, a first-aid kit, audio books on tapes or CDs, and road maps for all the areas through which they will be driving.

Letter of Authorization for Utility Company

Date: _____

Name of utility company: _____

Address: _____

City, state, zip: _____

Re: _____
<p style="text-align:center">(name of client; account number, if available)</p>

Property address: _____

To Whom It May Concern

I, the undersigned, hereby appoint _____ as my relocation agent, who is granted the authority to [transfer/close/initiate] the above-referenced utility services on my behalf.

I agree to pay all charges on the account once the service has been transferred or closed.

<p style="text-align:center">(OR)</p>

My relocation agent will submit the initial deposit required to begin service on the date of _____.

If there are any questions or if you need additional information, please do not hesitate to contact me at the address or phone number indicated below.

Dated this _____ day of _____, 20_____.

Account holder's signature: _____

Client's name: _____

Address: _____

City, state, zip: _____

Phone: _____

State of _____

County of _____

The foregoing authorization was acknowledged before me on this _____ day of _____, 20_____, by _____ (account holder), who is personally known to me, or has produced _____ as identification.

_____ Commission expires: _____
<p>Notary Public</p>

Auto Transport Services

Clients may ask you to make arrangements to have a car shipped or moved to the new location. Auto transport companies generally require two to three weeks' notice, and it can take up to ten days for the vehicle to arrive at the destination. When the car is delivered, someone must be present to inspect it and note any damage on the bill of lading. Be sure the driver or delivery agent signs and dates the delivery documents after you to indicate acknowledgment of the damage—otherwise, the auto transport company may not honor the claim. Be sure your client knows that it is against the law to put any personal belongings in the vehicle to be transported.

Movers

Some clients will select their own moving companies, but most will rely on you to find the best company to meet their needs. Finding a good, reputable moving company will be a challenge in itself, but when you do, it will be well worth the effort. When comparing moving companies, ask these questions before making your selection:

- Will they pack? If so, how much will they charge?
- Will they provide packing materials for you or your client to use? If so, how much will they charge?
- Will they dispose of boxes and packing materials after you unpack?

Movers and Shakers

To avoid the high prices of traditional moving companies and the hassles that come with the lower-cost approach of renting a van and doing the entire job yourself, some moving companies will provide a truck and moving equipment that you and your employees can load. Then one of the moving company's professional drivers will drive it to the designated location—local or long distance—where you will need to arrange to have it unloaded. Most of these companies also provide packing supplies and boxes for an additional fee.

If you have the manpower, "self-service moving" can be very cost-effective. You don't have to worry about providing your own moving van, hiring and insuring a professional driver, and paying for gasoline and maintenance on the vehicle. And you can use your own trusted employees for packing, loading, unloading, and unpacking.

- Will they provide a hand truck?
- Will they provide damage coverage?
- What is the total estimated moving cost?

Smart Tip

Put plastic bags around the hoses of washing machines, and secure them with rubber bands to prevent leakage while in transit.

Decide if you and your employees will pack all or some of the client's belongings yourselves or commission the moving company to do that task. Self-packing saves money, but letting the movers do it saves time and liability.

If the moving company packs, it is responsible for reparations if anything is lost or damaged. Typically, moving companies will pay up to 60 cents per pound for damage, loss, or breakage to furnishings and other household items. Some moving companies require that customers purchase additional insurance to cover damages that may occur during the move.

Before the movers arrive, dispose of toxic or flammable items like fireworks, cleaning fluids, aerosol cans, acids, and ammunition. Gas-powered machinery, such as lawn blowers, weed eaters, and snow blowers will need to be drained. For safety reasons, most movers will not transport flammable liquids.

When the movers arrive, go over all the details and paperwork, and verify delivery and payment arrangements. Commercial movers typically charge by the weight of the items on the truck and the distance they are being moved. Prior to arriving, the driver will have the truck weighed without anything in it, so make sure the movers provide you with an "empty weight" receipt as soon as they arrive.

Do a walk-through to take inventory with whomever is in charge. Point out the boxes you have designated to be loaded last and unpacked first. To avoid disputes after the move, the moving company usually has a moving inventory sheet that indicates the condition of the items being moved, which must be reviewed and signed by you or the client.

Once the truck has been loaded, give the van operator detailed directions to the new residence and include a phone number where you can be reached while they are in transit.

Have at least two people present when the moving van arrives at the new location: one to check the inventory sheets as items are unloaded, and the second to direct movers on where items are to be placed. You may want to have additional employees available to start unpacking as items are taken off the van, unless you plan on doing this after everything has been unloaded.

Research any possible delivery restrictions in advance so the movers know what to expect and can plan accordingly. For example, some communities only allow deliveries during certain times of the day, such as between 8:30 A.M. and 4:30 P.M. High-rise buildings may require dock space to be reserved in advance. Don't let the movers be surprised at the destination; that can cause delays and may result in additional fees.

If your client is moving to a multistory building, check to see if it has a freight elevator or at least a passenger elevator that will accommodate large pieces of furniture. If it doesn't, you'll need to arrange the necessary labor for the furniture to be carried up the stairs, and for larger pieces to be disassembled and reassembled.

Building managers and superintendents may also want to see the moving company's certificates of insurance proving that there is coverage to pay for damages if any occurs.

Make sure there will be suitable parking for the moving truck. If the truck has to double-park, the driver may have to drive around the block every so often to avoid getting a ticket, and that means additional charges.

Cleaning Services

At the old home, you can organize, clean, and help prepare the home for showing to prospective buyers, you can get it ready for a final walk-through or closing inspection, or you can do the final cleaning after your clients have moved out. Part of this cleaning can include removing trash and unwanted items. The trash can be picked up by the local garbage collectors or taken to the dump; anything useful can be donated to an appropriate charity for a tax deduction for your client.

At the new home, you can do a thorough cleaning before your clients arrive with their belongings. Wipe down walls and cabinets, clean and disinfect bathrooms and kitchen appliances, and vacuum and mop. The cleaning services section in Chapter 7 has more information about how to deliver this type of service.

> **Bright Idea**
> Have individual floor plans for each room in the house taped to the door of that specific room to help the movers know where to place the furniture. Be sure to put the name of the room on the floor plan to avoid any misunderstandings.

Use the Move Coordination Checklist on page 47 as a guide when assisting your clients with their relocation needs. Not every move will require every task on the list; adjust for the special circumstances of each project. Consider attaching the checklist as an addendum to your contract.

Sorting and Downsizing

Most of your clients will be moving from a larger home into something smaller and will need downsizing assistance. The apartments in retirement communities

Move Coordination Checklist

This checklist can be useful when helping your clients assess their relocation needs. You may want to attach it as an addendum to your contract.

At Contract Signing
❑ Contact real estate agent to assist with the sale of old residence.
❑ Contact real estate agent to assist with the purchase of new home.
❑ Provide client with documents.

Eight Weeks Prior to Move
❑ Draw a floor plan of new residence and decide what furniture to bring to new residence.
❑ Compare moving companies.
❑ Contact chamber of commerce or other local resources for newcomer information and packets.
❑ Process change of address for subscriptions.

Six Weeks Prior to Move
❑ Contact doctors, dentists, lawyers, accountant, and insurance agents and arrange to have records or information transferred.
❑ When possible and practical, identify new health-care providers (e.g., physician, hospital, pharmacy).
❑ Clean or repair furniture, carpets, curtains, or appliances, if needed.

Four Weeks Prior to Move
❑ Inventory, sort, and downsize household furnishings, closets, and cabinets.
❑ Hold an estate sale.

Three Weeks Prior to Move
❑ Make arrangements for travel, hotel, and pets.
❑ Properly service any automobiles that are driving a long distance.
❑ Arrange to have automobile shipped.
❑ Schedule connect and disconnect dates with utility companies.

Two Weeks Prior to Move
❑ Arrange to transfer bank accounts and safe deposit box contents to new branch locations or new bank.
❑ Process change-of-address notifications.
❑ Contact moving company to confirm arrangements.
❑ Cancel delivery services such as water and newspaper.

Move Coordination Checklist, continued

One Week Prior to Move
- ❑ Defrost and clean freezer and refrigerator.
- ❑ Line cabinet and closet shelves in new home.
- ❑ Change the locks on the new home.
- ❑ Research delivery restrictions so movers will not be surprised on moving day.
- ❑ Begin packing.
- ❑ Arrange to have "essentials" box and client's suitcase packed.

One or Two Days Prior to Move
- ❑ Arrange to have payment ready for moving company when they arrive.
- ❑ Make sure new residence is clean and ready for move-in.
- ❑ Test to make sure utilities are hooked up in new residence.
- ❑ Test smoke detectors in new residence.

On Moving Day
- ❑ Make sure all boxes are inventoried.
- ❑ Give movers detailed directions to new location, along with your cell phone number.
- ❑ Advise movers of any delivery restrictions.

Leaving the Former Residence
- ❑ Turn off water, lights, and appliances.
- ❑ Open refrigerator door if the electricity will be turned off.
- ❑ Turn off furnace, heat, or air conditioning.
- ❑ Lock all windows and doors.
- ❑ Conduct final inspection of all rooms, garage, attic, and basement.
- ❑ Remove all refuse.
- ❑ Surrender keys and garage door opener.

At the New Residence
- ❑ Tape a floor plan of the new home on the front door and individual floor plans on each room.
- ❑ Check off all items (furnishings and boxes) as they come off the truck.
- ❑ Unpack and set up bathrooms.
- ❑ Unpack and set up bedrooms.
- ❑ Unpack and set up kitchen.
- ❑ Unpack and set up living/family rooms.
- ❑ Unpack and set up remaining areas.
- ❑ Connect telephones, televisions, and lamps; set clocks.
- ❑ Remove refuse and packing materials.

are typically small, and the space in an assisted-living facility may be even more limited.

Create a floor plan of the client's new residence so she can start thinking about what furniture she can take and what will have to be sold or given away. Planning ahead of time how the furniture will be arranged in the new location will make the process of delivering the furniture easier. Use one of the many popular computer software programs that can quickly and easily create floor plans and furniture dimensions to scale, or do it with old-fashioned graph paper. Be sure to accurately measure everything your client is planning to take so you don't find out the hard way that something won't fit in the new home. Virtual furniture arranging is definitely easier than physically dragging a couch around a room.

In addition to deciding what furniture to keep, part of your downsizing efforts will be to thin out the contents of closets and cabinets. Many seniors have large collections of items that just aren't going to fit in their new residences. Karen Martin in Hartford, Connecticut, says, "Some clients need a de-cluttering either before the house goes on the market or just so they can see what is really left. Some people, especially seniors who lived through the Depression, have saved an awful lot of stuff, including plastic containers that really have no use. Sometimes all I am asked to do is remove all of the refuse."

Sorting must be done prior to packing and can take anywhere from a few days to a couple of weeks with an appropriate number of helpers. If you are doing this task on your own, depending on the size of the house you are downsizing, it could take anywhere from a few weeks to a few months. When going through books and papers, it's important to know what items should be kept and what needs to be tossed. In addition to her own knowledge, Martin also relies on independent contractors who are in the antique and collectible business or have a good knowledge of what things may have historical significance. "For instance, if there was a cruise line in the 1930s and you come upon one of their menus, don't throw that away. There are collectors for all sorts of paper goods, like sports memorabilia. I advocate recycling and not throwing away anything, especially items that have an interesting printed history."

In her book, *Gaining Control Over Home Downsizing: Inspirational Stories*, Martin writes, "Home downsizing, well planned, well organized, and well executed, can be one of life's most freeing experiences. Conversely, it can be physically exhausting, emotionally draining, and expensive." Not only does Martin provide practical tips and tricks to save time and money, she also offers emotional insight to help ease some of life's transitions.

If possible, have a family member sitting with the senior client when they are going through their personal things, especially papers and memorabilia. "What is so important to this process of moving forward with a positive attitude is reminiscing and having somebody who that person knows, a relative or a dear friend, to really listen, to capture the stories. There is a lot of history," Martin says. "So my emphasis is on the process, which is going to be difficult. There are going to be tears shed. There is going to be laughter. It is kind of like a life review. It is something that only happens at this time. Adult children or other relatives who can't be present to help an elderly person through this process really miss out. This is so important."

Keep a list of all the furnishings the client decides to keep, and note the estimated replacement costs for moving insurance purposes. If an item will be difficult to replace, make a note of it on the list and then take extra precautions when having it moved.

Once your client has decided what she's going to keep, you can arrange for the disposal of the remaining contents of the home. Family heirlooms may be shipped to various relatives, some useful items may be donated to your client's favorite charity, some things may be discarded and the remainder may be sold.

Estate Sales

Your clients may want to sell their unwanted but useful and valuable household furnishings and other items at an estate sale. Your first step is to get everything organized, tagged, and priced. Create an inventory of what is to be sold so you can quickly and easily check it off when the sale is completed. Then consider how you can display the goods to their maximum advantage.

When Martin sets up for estate sales, she covers large folding tables with cloths to create an attractive display of smaller items. She says that flat top strawberry boxes found at her local grocery store are great for sorting and displaying. "I have a way of setting up sales where the better items are in the living room and dining room, and then your household items are in the kitchen." Martin also uses antique drying racks for linens, and a unique metal rack with clips that was probably originally intended as a postcard holder to display old gloves or other special items. Be creative in finding and using innovative display tools and merchandising techniques to get the best prices for your clients.

One of the biggest concerns while holding an estate sale is security. Hundreds of people will be going through designated rooms, and sometimes the entire house. Consider the size of the house and have enough people on hand to help—some to assist with selling and others with collecting money. Martin says that she also has a worker who stands at the door and allows only a certain number of people into the home at one time. "That same person also checks the items as they leave [to make sure they've] been paid for. We have a system of communicating with receipts or stickers that something has been paid for," she says. "I have what I call an intake sheet, where we have clipboards and simple sheets that have a description of the item and the amount paid."

Promote your estate sales with yard signs and advertisements in the local newspaper. You should also build a mailing list of estate sale shoppers so you can send them a postcard announcing your sales.

As an alternative to estate sales, you may sell the items on consignment through a local auction house or consignment shop, through online auctions like eBay, or through your own auction website.

Packing

Packing is often one of the most challenging tasks for your senior clients. Some will want you to pack everything; others will just want you to pack specialty items. Do a walk-through and identify items that need special packing attention. Decide which items will be placed in storage and which will be sold or disposed of.

If you are doing the packing, you will need to provide the packing materials. For an additional fee, most moving companies will provide moving supplies such as packing tape, bubble wrap, and wrapping paper, as well as suitable boxes, especially ones designed for holding hanging clothes, glassware, and lampshades. You can also purchase supplies from local vendors or online (see Appendix for resources).

Begin the packing process with nonessential items, such as seldom-used dishware and cookware, curios, and decorative items, art, photographs, seasonal clothing, etc. Heavier items go in smaller boxes and lighter items get packed in larger boxes for easier lifting. The label on each box should include a detailed inventory of the box contents and indicate which room it belongs in at the new location.

Seal the bottoms of boxes with a strip or two of packing tape. Pack boxes firmly to avoid the shifting of contents during the move by placing heavier items on the bottom and lighter items on top. If you need additional padding, use old towels or linens, or crumpled paper. Records and CDs should be packed vertically in boxes, not flat.

Try to box things together that you will want to unpack first and label each box accordingly: "Open First—Load Last." This will be helpful when you arrive at the new residence and start unpacking your client's belongings. Essential items for these containers include cookware, dishes, glasses, tableware, bedding, linens, clothing, and toiletries.

It will be easier if you pack room-by-room, keeping similar items together. Put the hardware for disassembled furniture into a plastic bag along with assembly information, label the bag, and tape it to the furniture.

When packing, keep an eye out for frayed electrical cords on lamps, radios, and other appliances. Bring it to the client's attention and then make arrangements to have it repaired or replaced. Give the same consideration to any furniture that needs repairing, such as loose table or chair legs or broken bed slats.

> **Bright Idea**
>
> Wrap lampshades individually with clean, nonprinted packing paper. Stack two or three in a large box so they will stay clean and won't get crushed.

In the kitchen, discard any outdated cans of food. If you come across expired medications, alert the client so he can make arrangements to safely discard the drugs and update his prescriptions.

Offer to provide nonskid rug pads for area rugs to make them safer in your client's new home. Also make sure the rugs go on the truck last, so they will come off first to be placed on the floors under the furniture.

Items that will need special handling during the packing process include important documents such as birth certificates, wills, insurance policies, financial records, and stock certificates, photographs, home videos, and backup computer disks. These items should be transported personally by you or the client rather than in the moving van, or shipped by insured or certified mail.

Your client should also maintain possession of his checkbook, cash, or traveler's checks, medications, spare glasses, driver's license or identification card, automobile registration, insurance records, and health information. Help him pack a suitcase with comfortable clothing that will be kept accessible during the moving process.

Unpacking

Many of your clients will want their new homes completely ready for them to enjoy the moment they walk in, and will look to you for total unpacking and setup service. This includes hanging pictures and mirrors on the walls, setting up the kitchen and bathrooms, putting linens on the beds, stocking the pantry and refrigerator, plugging in the telephone, as well as removing any remnants of the move, such as boxes, bubble wrap, and packing peanuts.

When the movers arrive, it's helpful if the original packing team is waiting to begin unpacking as soon as boxes are taken off the truck. Their familiarity with the client's preferences and how things were set up in the former residence will be helpful as they unpack and put away.

Beware!
Before leaving his or her old home for the last time, remind your client to check for spare keys in all secret hiding places, with family members, or with the neighbor.

If the client doesn't want you to unpack everything in its entirety, at least have an "essentials box" ready for him when he arrives at his new residence to help him get settled. Some items to include are:

- Basic tools: hammer, screwdriver, wrench, pocketknife, and tape measure
- Paper supplies: cups, plates, napkins, paper towels, toilet paper, and trash bags
- Plastic utensils
- Flashlight, light bulbs, emergency candles, and matches
- Bath and dish soap
- Bottled water, instant coffee, tea bags, juice, or soft drinks
- Scissors, masking tape, utility knife, can opener
- Local phone books, pen and notepad, relocation packet with information about the area
- Telephone, radio, and batteries

Preparing the Home for Sale

Be prepared to offer your client the names of two or more reputable real estate agents they can talk to and select from. Some real estate agents will even give you a finder's fee if a homeowner signs a contract with them.

Make recommendations on what your client can do to increase the salability of the home. This could include landscaping and yard cleanup, paint, and repairs. Have a list of reliable handymen and contractors and offer to oversee the work if needed.

Once the house is ready to be shown, you can help stage it for the best results. Do this by decluttering, placing containers of fresh potpourri around the house, or accessorizing with colorful pillows. The client may also want you to be present when the house is being shown to prospective buyers. Realtors prefer that the owner is absent when they are showing a house; however, as a disinterested third party, you will not interfere with the sales process, and your client might feel more comfortable about having strangers in the house if you're there to keep an eye on things.

Choosing a New Lifestyle

Some clients will need your assistance to help them navigate through the maze of housing options. Often people are thrown into the situation of finding alternative housing without warning. Your services can save your client many hours of thumbing through the Yellow Pages, conducting online research, making phone calls, and mapping out locations.

▲

Help your clients assess their needs by first determining what level of assistance they need: no assistance required; part-time assistance with personal hygiene, taking medications, cleaning, or preparing meals; or full-time assistance due to dementia, prolonged illness, or loss of mobility. Other considerations will be cost range, anticipated time frame for moving, and desired area.

Retirement communities provide a variety of amenities, which will be another factor in helping your client decide where she would like to live:

- *Retirement communities* for active seniors usually offer spacious homes and villas rather than apartments. They also features amenities such as golf courses, swimming pools, clubhouses, and planned events with a program director.
- *Senior apartments and condos* are generally designed to be used by completely independent seniors. Amenities are more limited, but may include the use of laundry facilities and a swimming pool. Also, planned events and activities may be part of their program.
- *Assisted-living facilities* are usually studio-type apartments that provide housekeeping, meals, planned activities, as well as assistance with bathing, dressing, medications, and other daily living activities. Some may have special care for people suffering from Alzheimer's or dementia.
- *Continuing care facilities* offer apartments, villas, and sometimes houses for seniors to live in independently. Meals, housekeeping, and home and yard maintenance are usually provided. Most of these facilities also have a wide range of recreational activities. If one of the residents needs additional help with daily tasks, the facility will provide assisted-living services. And if a client needs 24-hour nursing care, that can also be provided on the premises, either in the resident's home or in the extended nursing care facility.

Not all your clients will be moving into a retirement community; some will want your assistance in moving into smaller homes, condos, or apartments that are easier for them to manage. Help them decide exactly what they want and where, then enlist the help of a qualified real estate agent in the desired area.

If your client is moving to a new community, suggest that he subscribe to the local newspaper in advance of the actual move. That will help him become familiar with the area and local events. Help him obtain anything else—such as a telephone directory, city map, dining guide. and other resource directories—that will tell him about his new home and make the adjustment as easy as possible.

Contact the town's chamber of commerce, economic development council, agency on aging, or senior community centers and ask if they have newcomer packets already prepared that include information on area attractions, shopping, churches, and entertainment.

What to Charge

Your fees may be per hour, per project, or commission-based. Often clients only need help with specific areas or tasks, so many senior relocation specialists offer a menu of services the client can choose from.

If charging by the hour, fees for senior relocation specialists are typically between $45 and $150 per hour, depending on the location and exactly what the client needs. If this is a large project requiring the assistance of one or more employees to sort through personal belongings, then you will also need to factor in their hourly rate when billing the client.

Have Pets, Will Travel

Relocating isn't just stressful for people but also for beloved pets. Planning is essential when pets are involved in the moving process, as they are usually sensitive to changes in their environment.

Moving companies will not move living things, including pets and plants. If your client is driving to his new home, his pet can ride along in the car, providing a greater sense of security for both the client and the pet during a stressful time. If he is traveling by air or train, help him arrange for transportation for the animal.

Consult with the client's veterinarian about medication or sedatives to reduce or eliminate motion sickness, agitation, and crying. Health documents regarding the pet will also need to be kept in a convenient place with the owner's other personal paperwork while on the road.

If the animal is small enough, it should travel in a pet carrier for safety reasons, even in a car. But if the pet is too big for a carrier, use a "doggy seatbelt," available in pet supply stores. This is a harness that attaches to a car's seatbelt and keeps the pet safely confined. Airlines and trains, of course, will have their own requirements for how pets are to be transported.

If you are making arrangements for your clients to stop overnight at a hotel or motel, you will need to find out in advance which ones will accept pets. Pack a travel suitcase for the pets that includes a leash for potty breaks, a water bottle, water, food dishes, a small supply of food and treats, and favorite toys. If it's a local move, arrange to have the client's pet stay with a friend or neighbor, or have the pet temporarily boarded at a kennel until the move has been completed.

Commission fees are based on a percentage of the client's household goods and furnishings that are liquidated, and are typically between 35 and 50 percent of the total sales. Martin says she uses a sliding scale when deciding what commission percentage to charge a client. "I first take into consideration how much stuff needs to be sorted and how many people I need to work with me," she says. "Then we see what the total sales are before calculating a final percentage. The higher the sales, the lower the commission."

Smart Tip

Remember to save all moving receipts and keep complete records of all related expenses for the client's accountant, because some or all of these expenses may be tax-deductible.

Martin bills her clients either by the hour or on commission, depending on what services are needed. "I bill the client per man hour, which is the case with a lot of my services, but if I am doing an on-site estate sale, or if I am liquidating in another way, I take a percentage of the total amount that I sell," she says.

Estate sale professionals usually charge a commission of 25 to 50 percent of the gross proceeds. The percentage is determined by taking into account the size of the estate, the amount of sorting, the research time involved in appraising the items, the quality of the furnishings, preparation for the sale, cleaning afterward, and the number of workers needed. Martin says, "If you have to go into every drawer and every closet, it is labor-intensive."

Equipping Your Operation

You don't need a lot of equipment to get your senior relocation business started. Depending on what you already own and the equipment needed for the services you want to offer, your required startup capital could range from just a few hundred to a few thousand dollars.

Martin said one of her biggest expenses was for 12 outdoor signs that she had specially designed to promote her estate sales. "The signs are in prominent colors of fuchsia and purple and really show up on the road," she says. "If somebody is driving by, the signs point them toward the estate sale." The signs are sturdy corrugated cardboard on metal bases, designed to be used repeatedly. Martin says her initial investment in signs was about $800 to $900.

All you really need is a car, but if you decide to add a moving van or truck with an enclosed cargo space to your operation, used ones can be found starting at $20,000, while a brand-new van could run up to $70,000 or more. You will also have to get adequate insurance, and make sure you have qualified drivers to operate the moving van.

Relocation Service Equipment and Supply Checklist

☐ 12 large moving boxes	$30–$50
☐ 3 wardrobe boxes	$38–$65
☐ 8 kitchen boxes	$30–$60
☐ 20 storage/book boxes	$15–$50
☐ 4 rolls packing tape	$12–$18
☐ 1 tape dispensers	$13–$20
☐ 1 roll (80 ft.) bubble wrap	$15–$45
☐ 1 box (25 lbs.) packing paper	$30–$60
☐ 3 bags packing peanuts	$17–$45
☐ 12 black markers	$12–$20
☐ 1 box cutter	$3–$10
☐ 1 hand truck/dolly	$35–$150
☐ 1 easel (estate sale display)	$25–$150
☐ 1 folding table (for display or packing)	$45–$100
☐ 350 stickers/labels (for pricing or labeling)	$10–$25
☐ floor plan design software	$80–$250

In addition to basic office equipment (see Chapter 13), use the Relocation Service Equipment and Supply Checklist above to get started. This list includes enough moving supplies for an average home; you may decide to buy more supplies than the amount indicated. If you have the cash, a place to store things, and can get bulk pricing, this will save you money in the long run.

Staffing

While it's possible to run a senior relocation business as a one-person operation, where you provide all the services to your senior clients as well as manage the company,

▲

it may not be practical—especially as you grow. There will most likely be times when you're going to need a reliable staff made up of independent contractors or full-time employees to help with sorting, packing, moving, and cleaning. Employees will need to be sensitive and understanding to the stress and anxiety that your clients may experience during this emotional time of upheaval. You may also find it helpful if staff members have a knowledge of antiques and collectibles. If you hold estate sales, you will need people to assist you with the preparation, pricing, and organization of inventory, followed by the removal of unsold items that are to be donated or recycled.

The mechanics of staffing—including finding, screening, and hiring employees; benefits; salary ranges; and other personnel issues—are discussed in Chapter 12. Address in detail how you will handle staffing your company in your business plan.

Special Designations and Organizations

Certified Relocation and Transition Specialists (CRTS)™ are trained professionals who provide specialized relocation services to assist mature adult individuals, as well as their families and/or caregivers throughout the entire moving process. These senior service providers understand the emotional and logistical issues their clients face which can include space planning, packing, sorting, organizing, and downsizing. To find out more about CRTS certification, visit the National Council for Therapeutic Recreation Certification (NCTRC) at www.nctrc.org.

It's also a good idea to join a professional organization for referral and networking opportunities. Two good ones are the National Association of Senior Move Managers (NASMM), www.nasmm.com, and the National Association of Professional Organizers (NAPO), www.napo.net. Both groups offer educational programs and resources. Being members of professional organizations gives you additional credibility, and you may be allowed to place their logos on your company's printed materials. Some also offer their members the option to participate in group insurance programs.

Stepping Stones

For many people, especially seniors, the relocation process can be overwhelming. As a senior relocation specialist, you will take the chaos out of moving, eliminate stress, and make the overall experience a positive one.

This step will be one of many in the aging process as older adults are faced with making lifestyle changes. Once they have resettled, another step may be bringing in home care or home health care to enable the senior adult to maintain a level of independence.

6

Home Care and Home Health-Care Services

By 2020, nearly 14 million people in the United States will be over the age of 85, and 84 percent of them will want to continue living at home. To do that, more than half will need assistance with daily living activities.

Seniors and family members of older relatives are looking at alternatives to assisted-living and nursing homes.

The best option for most is home care or home health care, where a professional caregiver goes to the home to personally look after a loved one. This may include doing laundry, picking up around the house, reading the newspaper out loud, and preparing meals. Most important, this service includes companionship—someone who adds conversation and friendship to the life of an elderly person who is homebound, physically impaired, has difficulty getting around, or may be lonely.

Depending on the level of care the client needs, a licensed medical professional may be required to administer medications, offer rehabilitative therapy, or provide other skilled nursing care.

This at-home alternative to institutional care is not only cost effective, but allows seniors to maintain a much-desired level of independence in familiar surroundings.

> ## Stat Fact
> According to the 2013 Cost of Care Survey by Genworth Financial USA, the average cost of a private room in a nursing facility is $230 per day. However, most Americans would rather receive in-home care because the one-on-one attention is generally better and the expenses are lower, costing an average of $150 per day. Because of this, Genworth says the demand for in-home care is on the rise and we face an impending caregiver shortage.

Home Care Services

Home care businesses are usually limited to nonmedical services. They are designed to assist individuals and couples who want to retain their independence by staying in their own homes with familiar surroundings.

Personal or home care aides provide a range of services that include companionship, meal preparation, light housekeeping, personal hygiene and grooming assistance, medication reminders, mail sorting, bill paying, and transportation to medical appointments or shopping.

Some states require formal certification and training for these individuals, while others do not. For states where there is no mandatory certification, aides can voluntarily apply for a national certification from the National Association for Home Care (NAHC) to indicate their willingness to meet the association's standards. Many states also offer non-mandatory certification courses for non-medical caregivers.

There are many benefits to becoming a certified in-home caregiver which include specialized training in CPR and first-aid, emergency preparation, end-of-life care, nutrition and meal planning, addressing legal issues regarding home caregivers, and learning how to work with the medical community. Plus, many long-term insurance companies will only recognize certified caregivers, which could be a major consideration if policy holders want to be reimbursed.

It's important to consider personality when matching a senior with a personal or home care aide. An introverted senior may feel more comfortable with someone who is low-key and has a gentle personality, while a livelier senior may prefer an aide who is more outgoing.

Home care services may be needed for a few hours a day or around the clock. Seniors who are new to the concept of home care may initially want to start with a slow transition into the service, perhaps with light housekeeping or transportation. As they feel more comfortable around their caregivers, they may use additional services, including companionship, personal grooming, and more.

A personal or home care aide's daily routine will vary by case. An aide may go to the same home every day for months, or even years. Most aides work with a

Match and Dispatch

To appropriately match home care or personal care aides with a senior client, you will need to ask specific questions:

- ○ Where will the home care take place?
- ○ Who is the primary contact person?
- ○ Who is the emergency contact person?
- ○ Is anyone else living in the household?
- ○ Are there any pets, and will they also need care?
- ○ Who are the client's medical professionals?
- ○ What is the client's height, weight, and date of birth?
- ○ What is the physical status of the client?
- ○ What is the mental status of the client?
- ○ Is the client on special medications?
- ○ Is the client ambulatory?
- ○ Is the client continent?
- ○ What specific duties does the aide need to perform (e.g., personal care, meal preparation, light housekeeping, laundry, transportation, companionship)?
- ○ What are the anticipated times this service will be needed? How many days a week and hours per day? Or will live-in service be required?

number of clients, typically visiting four or five clients for one to two hours each day.

Let's look at the specific services a home care business could offer.

Companionship

Companions provide mental stimulation by engaging their clients in conversation, playing cards or doing puzzles with them, taking them on walks or strolls, going out for meals or movies, or attending social or religious functions. Companions also help reduce clients' boredom, anxiety, and loneliness. Often, companions drive clients to medical appointments or social activities, or on shopping expeditions.

Lifestyle companions provide nonmedical assistance with the tasks of daily living, such as personal hygiene, bill-paying, light housekeeping, and meal preparation. Sometimes a companion may only need to visit for a few hours a day to check on things. Another client may want a companion to come in all day or all night.

If an around-the-clock companion is needed, assign a live-in companion with whom the client can bond. Or have the same three or four companions work in shifts, providing full coverage with the comfort of familiarity. Remember that live-in companions need their own quarters, ideally a bedroom with a small sitting area and private bath. And they'll need time off, so be sure that detail is addressed in your contract.

Night-care companions offer a degree of safety and comfort during the night, especially if the client tries to get out of bed or if there is an emergency. They will be on hand to assist a senior with bathroom care, medication, sleeplessness, or any other situation that might arise. Like live-in companions, they need a private place to sleep; even though their job is night care, it's unlikely they'll need to stay awake all night, every night. Their primary purpose is to be nearby and willing to assist if needed.

> **Bright Idea**
>
> Personal or home-care aides who provide live-in or night care may want to use a baby monitor so they can easily hear and quickly respond to their senior clients who awaken during the night.

A respite companion comes in to relieve the family caregiver for a few hours, overnight, or longer if needed. They carry out most of the same duties that a lifestyle companion does, including meal preparation, medication reminders, and companionship.

An in-hospital companion may sometimes be needed during the hours or days that family members cannot be with a hospitalized client. The companion can read to the client, take notes when the nurses or doctors come in, help feed the client if necessary, assist with other needs, and just generally be of comfort.

Meal Preparation

Getting seniors to eat regular, balanced meals can be a challenge. If dementia—even mild—is an issue, the client may have trouble identifying whether or not she is hungry. Sometimes medications will affect her appetite or taste sensitivity. If she is depressed, she may snack a lot and then not be hungry at meal times. Because many seniors have special dietary needs, careful and sometimes ingenious planning must go into meal preparation.

The aide will need to consider the client's tastes and preferences when planning meals. If a client likes food with a sweet taste, vegetables such as corn, peas, carrots, or acorn squash can be prepared. Broccoli or asparagus can be camouflaged with a cheese sauce. A baked potato plain, or stuffed with finely chopped meats or vegetables, is tasty and easy to swallow.

Though not all seniors have difficulty at meal times, the personal or home care aide should be ready for clients who do. In addition to preparing meals, the aide may also need to assist the senior with eating, especially if her motor skills have weakened due to illness or injury. Sometimes modified devices—such as utensils with wrist straps or thick handles for easier manipulation, or drinking cups with straws or handles—can be used to encourage independence and the ability to self-feed. Cut food into bite-sized pieces or prepare finger foods that are easy to eat. Soup can be served in a cup instead of a bowl to eliminate the need for a spoon.

Smart Tip

For a client with poor eyesight, use brightly colored plates, glasses, napkins, and placemats to create a high contrast. This will allow him to distinguish foods from nonfood items in front of him.

Medication Reminders

Personal and home care aides do not administer medications, but as part of their services they can remind the client when to take them. This can be done as part of the in-home service, or by calling the client on the phone.

The aide should make a list of all medications—prescribed and over-the-counter—and the times they are to be taken. The chart should be posted in a conspicuous place, visible to the client and family caregiver. Use the Medication Log on page 31 in Chapter 4 for this purpose.

Personal Hygiene and Grooming Assistance

Good hygiene promotes physical and emotional well-being and can be a great morale booster. But assistance in this area can be embarrassing or humiliating for the client. Aides should be taught how to treat clients with respect and help them preserve their modesty and dignity.

Sometimes the aide may only need to make sure the bathing area is safe and perhaps offer minimal assistance. Other times, clients may require transfer assistance by the use of a wheelchair or walker to a shower or tub that has safety handrails and/or a shower chair. Many states allow only certified medical personnel to provide assistance with transferring, lifting, and bathing; find out your state's

> ## Bright Idea
>
> If a client seems depressed or anxious, the aide can encourage her to put together a memory box with pictures and items representing happy times in her life, such as weddings, holidays, births, and other special events.

requirements before accepting clients who need this type of help. Oral hygiene is also important, and there may be times the senior client is unable to take care of this task herself. Tucking a towel under her chin and using a soft toothbrush while she is sitting up is preferable. But if she is bedridden, and state regulations permit it, the aide can still brush her teeth and gums by rolling her on her side or elevating her head.

Some clients will need assistance with dressing. That help may range from simply choosing a complete outfit and laying it out, to actually helping the client put the garments on. If your clients have difficulty with buttons or zippers, suggest acquiring clothing that can be pulled on or garments with snaps or Velcro™ fasteners.

Toileting is another issue that a senior client may need assistance with. Sometimes she may need help transferring from her wheelchair or walker to the commode. Other times she may require assistance cleaning herself. If she is incontinent, she will need to be taught how to wear disposable underwear or pads, and she may sometimes require assistance changing them.

Shopping, Errands, and Transportation

Home care aides can be available to run errands, such as picking up dry cleaning, prescriptions, library books, videos, and groceries, or doing a variety of other odd jobs. They can also escort their senior clients to medical appointments, the grocery store, or social or religious functions. Allen Hager, owner and founder of Right at Home in Omaha, Nebraska, says the aides employed by his company will be glad to drive the senior wherever he needs to go, but it has to be in the client's own car. Also, the client is required to sign a waiver releasing the company from any liability in the event of an accident while the aide is driving. His company always checks the driving records of its aides before sending them to a client's home.

If driving is part of an aide's job—even if it's just driving from client to client—you must check his or her driving record. And if your aides drive their own vehicles, they must be adequately insured.

If the client is wheelchair-bound or has other disabilities and cannot be transported in his or her own vehicle, contact your local Area Agency on Aging to see what special needs transportation might be available. You can also call the National Transit Hotline toll free at (800) 527-8279 for names of local transit providers who provide transportation to the elderly and people with special needs.

The Growing Need for Geriatric Massage

Geriatric massage is a specialized type of massage designed to meet the needs of senior adults. A properly trained massage therapist can help clients improve and maintain their overall well being, as well as sometimes regain certain physical functions that may have diminished due to the aging process. The elderly often suffer from poor blood circulation, arthritis, diabetes, and other age-related maladies. A geriatric massage therapist can gently manipulate the body's soft tissues to alleviate pain and increase range of motion. Many seniors are lonely and depressed, and massage therapy can be a wonderful technique to relieve gloominess and anxiety in touch-deprived clients.

Candy Malburg worked as a rehabilitation massage therapist for six years before learning of the tremendous need for therapists specializing in geriatric massage. "I did a lot of research on geriatric massage and went back to school to get specialized training for it," Malburg says. "Then I started doing research on the area's retirement communities and learned how to market to retirees."

Malburg believes that it takes a special kind of person to operate a business that caters to seniors. Some of the qualities needed to be successful in a senior service business are: reliability, patience, and sincerity. Another important quality is trustworthiness. "People are not only entrusting their care to you, but sometimes you have access to their homes and personal information," she cautions.

It also helps to be goal-oriented so that clients can see results and have a feeling of accomplishment. "Set goals for each visit," Malburg advises. "This will give your client something to work on until the next visit."

Light Housekeeping

Your aides can vacuum, dust, do laundry, change bed and bath linens, and generally tidy up around the house. For a more detailed description of cleaning services, see the "Cleaning Services" section in Chapter 7.

Administrative Services

Sometimes a senior client may need assistance with household bill management or filing insurance claims. Or he may need help with addressing and mailing greeting cards for holidays and special occasions, or want to send a letter to an old friend. An aide can prepare all of the paperwork for the client's or family caregiver's signature. See the "Administrative Services" section in Chapter 7 for more detail.

Home care (nonmedical services) should not be confused with home health care. Home health care is provided by licensed medical personnel and is typically operated as a separate business. However, you can combine the two services if you feel the demographics in your area will support them both.

> **Bright Idea**
>
> If a client has difficulty with vision or reading, instead of writing notes and reminders, the home care aide can record instructions on a tape recorder for the client to listen to after the aide has left for the day.

Home Health-Care Services

A home health-care business provides fully trained and licensed medical personnel for a variety of services to a senior in a home setting. If a client needs to have medication adjusted and administered, has wounds that need to be cared for, or needs vital signs and IVs monitored, he will need home health care.

Home health care costs significantly less than clinical or institutional care, which makes these services attractive and in demand. Candidates for home health care include people with chronic health problems, such as congestive heart failure, kidney or respiratory disease, or diabetes. Many terminally ill patients and their families prefer home health care to hospitals or institutional facilities. Families of Alzheimer's patients or cognitively impaired elderly people often seek home health-care services so their loved ones can remain in the security and comfort of their own homes.

Physicians will frequently discharge patients from the hospital sooner if there is a home health-care plan in place. When a client receives specialized patient care at home, both the client and the family are educated in the process. This helps to prevent exacerbations and repeat incidences of the disease, illness, or injury.

Because health issues vary greatly, so does the need for health-care visits. In some situations, a nurse may stop by the home only once a week to do a general health assessment and check the IV site. An occupational therapist may go to the home three times a week, and a certified nursing assistant may visit for a few hours every day to bathe the client and check vital signs.

The basic categories of home health-care services are discussed below.

> **Stat Fact**
>
> According to the National Center for Health Statistics, approximately 7.6 million individuals are currently receiving in-home care from 83,000 providers because of acute illness, long-term health conditions, permanent disability, or terminal illness. Additionally, annual expenditures for home health care are projected to be $57.6 billion in the coming year.

- *Basic nursing care* can be provided by a certified nurse's aide (CNA), who works under the direction of a nurse or physician. The aide typically performs many of the same services as a personal or home care aide, as well as measures and records vital signs and assists the client with bathing, dressing, and eating. A CNA does not dispense medications, check IVs, or do other invasive medical procedures.

- *Skilled nursing care* can be provided by a registered nurse (RN), a licensed practical nurse (LPN), or a clinical nurse specialist (CNS). Nurses can administer medications, check IVs, give injections, change bandages, take vital signs, and do general health assessments. Typically a nurse will visit several clients in a day; however, arrangements can be made for a client to have a live-in nurse, or nurses who regularly change shifts, so the patient will have around-the-clock care.

- *Wound care* may be needed due to a surgical incision, a specific injury sustained in an accident, or for bedsores that a patient suffered after a prolonged hospital stay. In addition to treating the wound and changing the bandages, the nursing specialist, such as an RN, LPN, or CNS, may educate the patient or family on how to care for the wound to help prevent complications.

- *General health monitoring* by a nursing specialist involves checking vital signs, such as blood pressure, blood sugar levels, cholesterol, and temperature. It may also include drawing blood under a physician's orders.

- *IV therapy* includes the monitoring of IV sites and lines on a routine basis. This type of service may include one or two visits per day or week. Often the patient or family caregivers can be taught how to put medications in the IV line, which can reduce the number of nurse visits and control costs.

▲

- *Rehabilitation therapy*, sometimes referred to as "in-home rehab," is an at-home program with services given by licensed physical therapists, occupational therapists, respiratory therapists, or speech pathologists in coordination with the client's own physician. These services are provided at home when circumstances—such as transportation or mobility issues, fatigue, or confusion—prevent the client from attending a traditional outpatient rehabilitation clinic. An in-home rehabilitation program often has better results because clients are more at ease in their own surroundings, and that means faster recovery.

What to Charge

The typical hourly rate billed for personal and home care aides is anywhere from $11 to $15 per hour, charged in half-hour increments. Home care is usually the easiest to bill because you are invoicing one set hourly fee regardless of the service performed. The daily charges for a personal or home care aide range from $88 to $120 a day, depending on how many hours the aide spends with the client.

All In the Family

Encourage family members to stay involved in your clients' lives, even if they live far away. They may need your guidance in knowing exactly what to do. Suggest that children and grandchildren be assigned specific times during the week to call their elderly relatives to remind them of something specific they need to do (such as take medications, exercise, feed the fish) or just to say "hello." Small children can make drawings that are mailed weekly to grandpa. The idea is to help the family stay connected and keep your client feeling supported and cared for.

Invite family members, neighbors, and friends who live nearby to frequently visit and help keep your clients' spirits lifted. In the absence of nearby family and friends, there are senior visitation programs that can be contacted through local churches or community centers that will assign volunteers to visit your client on a regular basis. There are also pet visitation programs that your client may enjoy. Not many people can resist a friendly lick from a canine visitor or a soothing purr from a cuddly feline.

For licensed medical professionals, the fees increase in accordance with the skill level of the professional and are also affected by the geographic area. For a certified nursing assistant, fees start at $12 per hour; for a licensed practical nurse, they begin at $20 per hour; and for a registered nurse, average fees are $32 per hour. Supplies are billed to the client separately.

Holiday rates of time-and-a-half should be charged on designated days such as New Year's Eve/Day, Memorial Day, Labor Day, Easter, Independence Day, Thanksgiving, and Christmas Eve/Day.

If you decide to accept insurance, those rates may differ from the private pay rates you establish. You will need to investigate what eligibility criteria your operation has to meet before you can receive insurance benefits. The major sources of funding for home health-care services are Medicare, Medicaid, private insurance (Medigap, long-term, personal health insurance), and out-of-pocket.

> **Tip...**
>
> **Smart Tip**
>
> Have adequate security controls in place. For instance, employees should wear photo identification badges when they go to a client's home. If an aide does personal shopping or errand services for the client, it's recommended that she doesn't carry the client's cash. Instead use a limited-access credit or debit card, or give the client a receipt for reimbursement.

Equipping Your Business

In addition to office space and basic office equipment, probably the most important thing for your home care or home health-care business is computer software. Right at Home's Hager recommends purchasing software created for home health-care businesses that lets you effectively bill clients for services rendered, pay vendors, monitor and track the scheduling and staffing of your care providers, and efficiently maintain all your business records.

Comprehensive software like Hager describes can cost from $6,500 to $25,000, depending on the services needed. Most software companies have monthly payment plans or leasing arrangements that can be used to offset the cost. Programs you may want to consider include those offered by TimeTrack and PRN Plus; see the "Equipment, Supplies, Software, and Services" section in the Appendix for contact information.

For a home care business, very little is needed in the way of inventory and supplies. For a licensed home health-care operation, you'll need provisions such as bandages, gloves, and other medical supplies. Please see the Home Health-Care Supplies Checklist on page 70 for suggested items.

Home Health-Care Supplies Checklist

❑ 1 large bottle cleanser/lotion	$5–$13
❑ 1 bottle hand sanitizer	$2–$7
❑ 1 box latex gloves	$6–$12
❑ 1 pill dispenser/organizer	$3–$12
❑ 1 case disposable underwear	$50–$75
❑ 1 first-aid kit	$15–$150
❑ 1 box assorted bandages	$3–$12
❑ 1 bottle antiseptic	$2–$20
❑ 1 ear thermometer	$25–$180
❑ 1 blood pressure cuff	$16–$100
❑ 1 stethoscope	$50–$250

Contingency Plans

Your clients depend on the aides or nurses you have assigned to care for them, but there will be times when an employee will be unable to get to the client's home due to vacation, illness, inclement weather, or other reasons. Have a backup plan in place so your clients are not without care.

Remember to develop policies and procedures that protect the privacy and safety of your clients, as well as your employees.

Staffing

You will need to hire properly credentialed companions, aides, and nurses, either on a part- or full-time basis, or as independent contractors. Your staff-to-client ratio will depend on the services you offer, the needs of your clients, and the geographic area you are covering. As you grow, you'll need a receptionist, a scheduling coordinator, and a bookkeeper, in addition to more care providers.

How you will handle staffing your company should be addressed in detail in your business plan. The mechanics of staffing—including finding, screening, and hiring employees; benefits; salary ranges; and other personnel issues—are discussed in Chapter 12.

7

Concierge
Service

In the corporate world, concierges are often referred to as personal assistants. They perform a wide range of services for clients. A concierge who targets seniors performs many similar functions, only with a twist: Their mission is to enrich the lives of their elderly clients by delivering services that allow those clients to maintain an independent, dignified lifestyle as long as possible. And in many cases, they simply provide a warm, human touch for an older person who feels lonely and isolated.

Seniors turn to concierges for things they can't or don't want to do for themselves, or for companionship that is not available elsewhere.

Some of the concierge services you may provide include:

- Companion/support
- Administrative assistance
- Organization of closets, cabinets, basement, attic, garage, or filing system
- Errand and courier service
- Mail delivery and pickup (if mailbox is not at residence)
- Grocery shopping
- Personal shopping
- Fitness training
- Computer training and support
- Daily checkups
- Reminder services
- Cleaning services
- Pet care services
- Meal preparation

Many concierge services concentrate on one or two specialties, while others offer a wider range of services. Decide what tasks you would enjoy doing and then do a market study to determine if sufficient demand exists. From there you may find that your business can expand to include other services to better meet your clients' needs. And if you are unsure about your direction, start small with one or two basic services that can be expanded as the need demands.

When Dick Padgett started his Five Star Concierge business in San Diego, his primary service was transportation. But as his clients came to know and trust him, they relied on him more and more for other things like various household odd jobs, computer setup and training, and special projects such as organizing closets, garages, and filing systems.

As you decide what services your concierge business will offer, consider how one will blend with another. For example, companion services go well with administrative or cleaning services; transportation and personal shopping make a good match, as do handyman and window washing, and errands and pet services. The idea is that once you have a client, it's easier to increase the amount of business you are getting from someone who already likes and trusts you than it is to find a completely new client. And if your range of services has a logical connection, it will be easy to persuade your clients to use you more.

Companion Services

Paid companions can provide a great deal of comfort and a wide variety of services to elderly clients who are homebound, need help getting around, or who want assistance they can rely on. A client may need these services for a few hours a day or around the clock.

Companions perform a wide range of functions, including:

- Household budgeting and bill-paying
- Light housekeeping
- Assisting clients with bathing and personal grooming
- Running errands
- Escorting clients to and from medical appointments
- Meal preparation
- Writing correspondence
- Reading books, letters, and other material to the client
- Laundry and ironing

Some seniors may just need someone to come in one or two days a week for a few hours to visit and check on things. Others, especially seniors who may have memory impairment, may need someone to be on hand 24 hours a day, seven days a week.

The different types of companion services you could offer are:

> **Smart Tip**
>
> Start your concierge business out small; test your market and operation slowly before expanding. It's easier to correct small mistakes than large ones.

- *Lifestyle companion.* This professional offers nonmedical assistance with daily tasks, including personal grooming, housekeeping, and meal preparation. This arrangement could be for a few hours a week or as a live-in companion.
- *Companion escort.* This person would accompany the client to medical appointments or when running errands.
- *In-home respite companion.* This is the equivalent of an adult sitter to relieve the family caregiver for a few hours or overnight.

▲

- *Travel companion.* Active seniors who need transportation and someone to accompany them when visiting parks, museums, theaters, and other places might require a travel companion.

See Chapter 6 for more detailed information on nonmedical home care or companion services.

Administrative Services

Judy Heft of Stamford, Connecticut, started her business, Judith Heft & Associates, LLC, in 1996 to assist seniors with paying their bills and other administrative tasks.

Certifiably Humane

There are currently no certifications specifically for a personal concierge; however, you can obtain certifications within specialty areas, such as a personal chef, personal fitness trainer, or personal assistant. Certifications give you credibility and indicate that you have specific knowledge and skills. Belonging to professional organizations and associations will indicate to your clients that you are operating within the highest standards of your profession and keeping informed of current trends. The National Concierge Association (NCA) provides networking, educational, and promotional opportunities to its members, and offers an NCA Certified Concierge designation to qualified applicants within its organization. Visit nationalconciergeassociation.com for details.

You can also expand your knowledge and skills by participating in online classes that are tailored for people who want to learn more about operating an errand or concierge business. While these are noncredit courses, they do offer certificates and awards on satisfactory completion of the class. To find a list of available courses, start by doing an online search, typing "errand business class" or "concierge business class" in the search box. Universal Class (universalclass.com) is one of several online learning institutions where you can find these types of classes.

In addition to the above, special certifications may sometimes be awarded to your business by other associations and organizations, such as small-business associations, minority organizations, or related groups. For instance, if your business is owned and operated by a woman, you may be eligible for a certificate from the Women's Business Enterprise National Council.

She knew there would be a huge need for her services as the senior population was starting to show significant growth.

Her business helps monitor clients' financial affairs and make sure no one else takes advantage of them. "Theft by caregivers is a problem I sometimes run into, as well as theft by the client's children who have a feeling of entitlement." Heft says charitable organizations also take advantage of seniors by sending little gifts such as address labels, calendars, and blankets. This makes the seniors feel obligated to send the organization money they can't afford. Or the minute the organization gets the contribution they come right back asking for more money. "If careful records aren't kept, the seniors forget and send out another check."

If you provide administrative services for seniors, you'll enjoy a great deal of variety and flexibility in your work. Depending on the specific services you offer, you can work from home, at your clients' homes, or from a commercial location with employees.

The administrative services you can offer to seniors include:

- Handling their business and personal correspondence
- Setting up and organizing a filing system for personal or business papers
- Addressing and mailing holiday, special occasion, and thank-you cards
- Picking up and delivering the mail if their post office box is not at their residence
- Assisting with banking, including making deposits, writing checks, and paying bills
- Filing insurance claims
- Photocopying
- Notarizing
- Planning events for special occasions, dinners, and parties
- Organizing a reminder service for special occasions
- Making assurance calls (calls to clients to check on them)

You can bill by the hour or by the project. Hourly rates will be contingent on demographics and the complexity of the service you are providing, and typically range between $25 and $50 per hour. If you prefer to bill for individual projects, you still need to estimate how much

Smart Tip

Don't do all the running around yourself. Coordinate with a mobile dry cleaning service to pick up and drop off laundry. Contact a reputable grocery store that will deliver your orders. Find a reliable courier service that will pick up and drop off documents and packages.

time you anticipate a specific task will take. For instance, if you are addressing 50 holiday greeting cards, and you predict that it will take a maximum of three hours to complete this assignment, you might set a fixed fee of $45. In either case, keep accurate time records; if you're billing by the project, you'll want to be able to periodically evaluate your profitability, and to do that you'll need to know how long the project took.

You'll also need to decide how you will bill for travel time, mileage, supplies, and incidentals. You may set your hourly rate high enough to absorb those costs, or you may invoice for them separately.

Many of the services you'll offer to seniors are similar to those offered by a business support service. For more information on starting this type of business, see Entrepreneur's *Start Your Own Business Support Service*.

Personal Shopper and Errand Services

If you enjoy shopping and hate being tied to a desk, consider personal shopping or errand services. It's a bonus if you're a bargain-hunter; many of your senior clients will appreciate it if you find them good deals.

Under the umbrella of personal shopping and errands, you can:

- Pick up and deliver library books, video, and DVD rentals, dry cleaning and laundry, and prescriptions
- Pick up and deliver mail, ship small packages, purchase stamps and other mailing supplies
- Pick up and deliver documents to doctors and law offices, landlords, or tenants
- Shop for and put away groceries and other household supplies
- Shop for clothing, personal items, and gifts
- Wrap gifts
- Handle banking tasks
- Take clients' cars for service, repair, and DMV inspections
- Provide eldercare checks
- Coordinate household repairs

> **Bright Idea**
> Offer gift certificates for concierge services. They can be purchased in hourly increments (usually with a two-hour minimum) for grocery shopping, administrative services, meal preparation, companion/sitter service, light housekeeping, or laundry. As the client or family caregiver sees the convenience of these services, often these short-term assignments will expand into longer-term relationships.

Bright Idea

When you are on a personal shopping mission for a client, use an instant or digital camera to take pictures of items you have found before you buy. This allows your client to be involved in the purchasing decision without having to go to the store.

Organization Is Key

Staying organized is critical for personal shoppers and errand services. Consolidate trips so that one visit to the supermarket or drugstore can meet the needs of several clients. Respect your clients' privacy, and don't let one client know what you're doing for another.

When you are running errands or shopping for multiple clients at once, set up plastic or cardboard boxes in your vehicle marked with each client's name. After you purchase or pick up items, place them in the appropriate container. Keep a separate folder or envelope for each client's receipts.

Grocery shopping, in particular, takes a tremendous amount of planning and organization, especially if you are doing it for more than one person. Choose one or two days of the week for grocery shopping, and have your clients fax, phone, or email their lists to you the day before.

Pay for each customer's grocery order separately so you can provide individual receipts. After the clients' orders are bagged, make sure to write their names on the bags for easy identification and to avoid any delivery mix-ups.

What to Charge

You can charge for errand and personal shopping services by the hour, by the project or assignment, or by the mile. When dealing with big-ticket items such as furnishings and electronics, some personal shoppers charge a percentage of the amount of the purchase. Keep track of parking fees and tolls; you may bill these expenses back to your clients or set your rates high enough to absorb them.

Decide if you want to set up a regular and after-hours rate structure: Will you offer your services 24 hours a day, seven days a week, or have specific hours, such as 9 A.M. to 5 P.M.? How much notice will you require before something becomes an "emergency" errand with appropriate surcharges?

In the errand industry, how you bill your clients is still a gray area with no preset guidelines. Some errand services bill for services on a weekly, bimonthly, or monthly basis. Others

Smart Tip

Keep a mini-cassette tape recorder on hand to record notes to yourself while you are running around town.

The Price Is Right

In the concierge industry, there are no rigid rules on how to charge your clients. Instead, there are different billing strategies you can consider using in your business:

○ *Monthly retainers.* Family caregivers may prefer this method of paying in advance for services (example: $150 for six hours of service). When the client is close to using up the amount of time that has been prepaid, you can alert the client or caregiver so he can make a decision whether to pay for extra time or not use your services until the beginning of the next month. Decide how you'll handle the situation of a client having time left over at the end of the month; either roll those hours over to the next month or simply start fresh.

○ *Hourly.* Typical rates are anywhere from $25 to $125, depending on your location and the services you provide.

○ *Per task.* Create a list of the services you provide and the cost of each. For example, you may charge $2 per assurance call or $35 to take a client to and from the doctor's office.

○ *Membership fees.* This is a variation of the retainer concept. Offer various "membership" levels (e.g., gold, silver) that include a specific number of requests or hours per month for an annual, quarterly, or monthly fee. For example, a basic membership plan could be $50 a month for three hours of service. Or a premium membership plan could be $1,500 a year, allowing for up to eight hours of service a month, with additional hours billed separately. These plans would be offered as cost-effective alternatives to paying as you go.

charge membership or retainer fees that allow a predetermined amount of requests or hours. Another alternative is to ask for payment at the time you provide your services.

For shopping services, you can arrange for your clients to pay for the items you purchase in advance with a cash advance or a limited-access credit or debit card. If a client wishes to use a personal check, the store can be contacted in advance to get the total amount, including tax, or, if they are comfortable doing so, they can give you a signed check made payable to the store and leave the amount blank. Many concierges prefer not to handle the client's money and will present the client with a receipt for reimbursement on delivery or bill for those expenses in the next invoice.

Many of the services you'll offer are similar to those provided by a personal concierge. For more information, check out Entrepreneur's *Start Your Own Personal Concierge Service*.

Cleaning Service

As we age, many household chores become increasingly challenging. Even seniors who are still physically capable of housework may prefer to let someone else do it.

Beware!
Always use caution when cleaning around computer equipment, especially when using chemicals. Many monitors have an anti-glare coating that should not be cleaned with ordinary glass cleaner. Instead, use a product for cleaning computer monitors.

A typical cleaning service for seniors includes dusting, vacuuming, cleaning fixtures, mopping floors, wiping counters, and making beds. Additional services could include window and wall washing, carpet cleaning, floor buffing, and cleaning attics, basements, patios, or balconies. Present your clients with a list of cleaning services that are included in your basic fee, and then a separate list of tasks that you will do for an additional fee. Use the Cleaning Checklist on page 82 as an example.

In addition to regularly scheduled housekeeping, cleaning services may also include one-time events such as a spring cleaning of the house, basement, garage, or attic. You can also offer cleaning services to take place prior to or immediately following a move to a new location. If relocation services are not part of your concierge operation, then cozy up to a senior relocation and moving company (see Chapter 5) so they can call on you when needed. Light housekeeping services may also be incorporated as part of home care or companion services, which are covered in Chapter 6.

Window washing could be a specialty niche or another service included as part of your cleaning service operation. The only tools you need for this job are a ladder, squeegee, bucket, and bottle of ammonia. Window cleaning is often more than just removing dirt if the windows have tape or glue on them, or have been painted over. Some window cleaners charge by the pane, typically $1 to $3 each, depending on how many stories the residence or building has. Others charge by the job, using an hourly labor rate of $15 to $25.

An important requirement for the owner and employees of any type of cleaning service is honesty and discretion. Your clients must be able to have complete trust in the people who are coming to their homes. Also, from time to time you will undoubtedly be privy to personal information; safeguard your clients' privacy and never

Cleaning Checklist

REGULAR CLEANING

Bathrooms
- [ ] Toilets cleaned and disinfected
- [ ] Tile walls rinsed/wiped
- [ ] Bathtubs cleaned and disinfected
- [ ] Vanity and sink cleaned and disinfected
- [ ] Chrome fixtures cleaned and shined

Dusting
- [ ] Furniture dusted
- [ ] Glass table tops, mirrors, and doors cleaned with glass cleaners
- [ ] Windowsills, blinds, and ledges feather-dusted
- [ ] Light fixtures and lampshades feather-dusted
- [ ] Picture frames feather-dusted

Kitchen
- [ ] Clean front of appliances
- [ ] Interior clean of microwave
- [ ] Interior clean of toaster oven
- [ ] Spot-clean cabinets
- [ ] Interior clean of refrigerator

Floors
- [ ] Floors vacuumed/swept
- [ ] Mop tile/wood floors

Miscellaneous
- [ ] Bed and bath linens changed
- [ ] Sweep patio/porch
- [ ] Water plants

COMPREHENSIVE CLEANING

Bathrooms
- [ ] Clean tile walls and grout
- [ ] Wipe door frames and walls
- [ ] Faces of cabinets wiped with damp cloth
- [ ] Baseboards wiped

Dusting
- [ ] Windowsills and blinds wiped
- [ ] Furniture polished
- [ ] Knickknacks hand-washed
- [ ] Baseboards hand-wiped with damp cloth
- [ ] Pictures dusted and glass wiped with window cleaner

Kitchen
- [ ] Faces of cabinets wiped with damp cloth
- [ ] Scrub drip pans under burners
- [ ] Clean and shine appliances
- [ ] Clean top and sides of refrigerator
- [ ] Kitchen furniture hand-wiped
- [ ] Clean stove

Floors
- [ ] Shampoo carpets (if needed)
- [ ] Extra attention to cleaning corners of floors

Miscellaneous
- [ ] Doors and ledges vacuumed
- [ ] Lampshades vacuumed
- [ ] Carpet edges vacuumed
- [ ] Vacuum under accessible furniture
- [ ] Cobwebs removed

repeat confidential information. If you see personal papers lying about or come across evidence of other delicate matters, pretend you didn't see it—unless someone's safety or welfare is at risk.

An important element in the cleaning industry is appearance. Cleaners who are well-groomed and wear neat, professional-looking uniforms elevate their self-esteem, as well as the image of their business.

Cleaning Business Basics

A cleaning service business can be started with very little cash, although the more capital you have, the greater your options are. The only major piece of equipment you'll need is a vehicle so you can get to your clients. You need the same equipment that you would use to clean your own home—and chances are, you already own just about everything you need. The essential cleaning supplies are: vacuum cleaner, mop, broom, dustpan, all-purpose cleaner, glass cleaner, and rags. Even if you have to buy everything new, you probably won't spend more than $350 for a one- or two-person operation. Also, many small cleaning operations opt to use their customers' supplies and equipment, and charge only for labor.

You can charge by the hour or by the job. You may charge an extra fee for the initial cleaning. A few phone calls to existing cleaning services in your area will tell you what the market rates are. For more on starting a cleaning business, see Entrepreneur's *Start Your Own Cleaning Service*.

Personal Chef Service

If you enjoy cooking, consider becoming a personal chef. Personal chefs are different from private chefs in that they are available for hire by anyone, while a private chef works only for one individual or family. Your personal chef service can offer affordable, delicious, healthy meals that are prepared in the comfort of your clients' homes, relieving them of the burden of shopping and cooking.

Personal chefs are hired to prepare a specific number of meals for individuals or their families on a prearranged "cook date." This will be the day you and the client have decided for you to come to her home and prepare meals in advance. Typically, you will schedule only one cooking session per day, during which you will prepare several meals to be stored and frozen for future consumption. Depending on your clients' preferences, you can schedule cook dates once a week, twice a week, or twice a month.

Stat Fact

According to the American Personal and Private Chef Association, the number of private chefs/household cooks is over 9,000 serving approximately 72,000 customers. During the next five years, this industry is predicted to more than double within the United States.

Menu Consultation and Preparation

Initially, you will meet with your clients or their caregivers to learn their individual needs, dietary concerns, and food preferences so that you can plan menus for them. You may even want to meet with their doctors to better determine their needs and restrictions.

Be prepared to provide sample menus that will show your creativity in offering meals that are both varied and well-balanced. Your sample menus should also feature diabetic, vegetarian, low-sodium, dairy-free, and kosher meals.

On the cook date, bring all your own equipment, including bowls, spoons, pots, pans, and cutting boards. Once the meals have been prepared, store them in uniform, disposable containers that you provide. Leave detailed heating instructions for your client or the caregiver. Then clean up, put everything away, and leave the kitchen area just as it was when you arrived.

Paw-sitive Pet Services

Pets make wonderful companions for seniors, but your clients may need help caring for their furry friends. As part of your concierge operation, you could offer the following pet-related services:

- ○ Provide fresh food and water.
- ○ Take pets on daily walks.
- ○ Provide limited grooming (bathing, brushing, etc.).
- ○ Clean litter boxes.
- ○ Clean bird cages.
- ○ Feed fish.
- ○ Give pets needed medications.
- ○ Provide transportation to vet or groomer with wait service.
- ○ Pick up and deliver pet food and supplies.

Written Expectations

A simple service agreement for each cook date should be signed by both you and the client or caregiver. The agreement should specify what services will be provided, the service fee, and who is paying for the supplies. Typically, the client will pay for the groceries when you provide a receipt. The contract should also state your cancellation policy. Do you want five days' notice or 48 hours' notice? And if the client misses that window, what do they have to pay?

Although some folks may initially wince at the cost of hiring a personal chef, you can convince even budget-conscious seniors of the cost-effectiveness of using your services. During the sales process, be prepared to justify your rates. Point out how much time and money is spent dining out and ordering takeout. And if your prospective clients are cooking their own meals, ask them to consider how much time they are spending at the grocery store and later preparing the food. For clients who don't drive, your service eliminates the cost of taxis or other public transportation, or the need to depend on family and friends to get to and from restaurants and stores.

What to Charge

You have a choice of pricing structures, so choose the one that works best for you and your clients. You may want to charge a set fee for a specific number of entrée portions, including appropriate sides, or per individual serving, plus the cost of the food. Or you can charge by the hour, plus the cost of food.

For example, you can charge $250 to prepare five complete frozen meals for two people, plus the cost of ingredients. Or you can charge $35 an hour for the time it takes you to shop and cook, plus the cost of food.

Some personal chefs require their clients to prepay, while others may ask for a 50 percent deposit. Food should always be billed separately because of the variability of the expense.

> **Dollar Stretcher**
>
> Form a purchasing group with other homebased small businesses to buy large quantities of supplies. This lets you to take advantage of bulk pricing.

Certifications

You do not have to be a dietician, nutritionist, or even a certified chef to offer personal chef services, but you need to have some knowledge in these areas to be successful.

Only one out of five personal chefs has a Certified Personal Chef (CPC) designation. Although it is not required, a specialized certification through a professional organization such as the United States Personal Chef Association or American

Personal Chef Association will give you more credibility. The CPC designation indicates that you have a minimum of two years' working experience as a personal chef, that you have documented continuing education within the field, that you operate within the Personal Chef Code of Ethics, and that you have successfully passed the food-handling safety program. To retain your membership, most personal chef associations require that you maintain liability insurance coverage; many clients will see this as a benefit.

Senior Fitness Training

Senior fitness training is one of the fastest growing segments of the personal fitness training industry. Aging Americans are seeing the value of getting in shape and are doing something about it. Plus, doctors and managed care organizations have recognized that diet and exercise are an important part of keeping people healthy and reducing health-care costs.

Stat Fact
Research by the National Institutes of Health (NIH) indicates that older people who exercise regularly are more likely to remain independent than those who don't. Other research conducted by the NIH shows that positive changes in exercise habits and diet can reduce the risk of diabetes in high-risk seniors by 71 percent.

In some cases, a well-planned fitness program that uses light weights can help a senior gain enough strength to stop using a walker or wheelchair. Even after years of a sedentary lifestyle, an elderly man or woman can develop a physically active way of life through strength training and exercise.

This is where you come in. Older folks need to learn special training and fitness techniques that are complementary to their conditions. Sometimes exercises will be done while seated in a wheelchair or standing behind a regular chair for balance. Some personal trainers work with people who have suffered an illness or injury and need assistance transitioning back to a physically active lifestyle. This is an area known as "clinical exercise" and is an important part of the rehabilitation process. Trainers work in conjunction with their clients' medical doctors and physical therapists to establish appropriate exercise programs; then they assist clients as necessary to implement the programs.

What Do Personal Trainers Do?

Personal trainers work with senior clients who need instruction and coaching in different areas, including exercise physiology, kinesiology, nutrition, fitness assessment, exercise programming, cardiovascular exercise, flexibility techniques, and more.

They usually work with individuals one-on-one, but they also work with pairs and small groups.

Personal trainers can visit clients at their homes, fitness centers, rehabilitation centers, or anywhere else someone might need help, while earning $45 to $150 or more per hour.

Depending on how you set up your business or design your specialty, your clients will stay with you anywhere from a few sessions to a few years. Some trainers carefully seek out long-term clients; others choose a niche where they educate a client about fitness, or work them through a rehabilitative process, and then move on.

Senior services typically offered by personal trainers include:

- Fitness assessments
- Individual exercise programs
- Individual weight/fat-loss programs
- Nutrition consulting
- Strength and endurance training
- In-home personal training
- Cardio/respiratory programs
- Flexibility exercises
- Individual or small group training
- Seminars and classes on fitness and nutrition

Certifications

Certifications are important because they indicate that you have a certain level of knowledge and skill in your area of specialty. Although there are no professional licensing requirements for personal trainers, other certifications you may want to consider earning include:

- Aerobic fitness trainer
- Aqua fitness trainer
- Certified fitness advisor
- Certified personal trainer
- Clinical exercise specialist
- First responder/first aid
- Fitness therapist
- Group fitness instructor
- Lifestyle and weight management consultant
- Performance nutrition specialist

- Personal defense specialist
- Rehabilitation exercise specialist
- Senior fitness specialist
- Specialist in fitness for the physically limited
- Strength and conditioning specialist

These certifications can be obtained by joining professional organizations that offer qualifying educational programs as well as ongoing support services. There are literally hundreds of organizations that provide courses on anatomy, exercise physiology, and other aspects of personal training. Some of these professional associations are listed in the Appendix; however, many more can be found by conducting an internet search.

The U.S. Department of Labor Bureau of Labor Statistics offers an occupational handbook for recreation and fitness workers at bls.gov/oco/ocos058.htm. This handbook discusses certification and educational requirements for these fields, as well as competition and job prospects for fitness trainers.

Getting Started

Perhaps the easiest and least expensive way to start your personal senior fitness training business is as a homebased operator training with clients at their locations: homes, offices, or fitness centers. If you are going to offer fitness training at your home, it's best if you can set up a dedicated workout room, but a clear space in your living room will suffice. Startup costs for a trainer who works with clients at home or their locations can be as low as a few hundred dollars, depending on what office and exercise equipment you already own. If you want to invest in a commercial facility, you will need anywhere from $50,000 to $150,000 to furnish and equip your operation.

As increasing numbers of seniors become comfortable using computers, you may find a market for cyber fitness training and offer online training programs. Clients can use your website to complete forms that will let you conduct an assessment and create a training schedule for them. You can provide them with an online exercise journal, which you review regularly to evaluate their progress and make adjustments if necessary. Questions can be handled through email. This can be a cost-effective plan for clients who may not be able to afford a face-to-face fitness program. Although you would typically charge 40 to 60 percent less than a traditional trainer, you could increase your profits significantly because you would be able to take on more clients at one time.

Another popular trend is taking your program on the road by outfitting a van or recreational vehicle with exercise equipment and bringing the gym to your clients' homes or to a senior community. Generally, a mobile studio costs less than half of a small commercial storefront-type studio, with your biggest expense being the vehicle. You might also check with a rehabilitation or senior fitness center to provide personal training services in their facility.

Do thorough market research to see what type of fitness program would best be supported in your area. Learn more about the business of personal training in Entrepreneur's *Start Your Own Personal Training Business*.

Computer Basics

The golden age of the web is upon us: Seniors (age 64 to 75) represent the fastest-growing segment of internet users, clearly proving that you can indeed teach an old dog new tricks. These days, eyebrows no longer lift in amazement at the thought of senior citizens going online. In fact, they are heading into cyberspace in droves to access information on education, health, genealogy, hobbies, and more. Plus, online communication has proved to help the older population reduce isolation by staying in touch with family and friends.

Some seniors are initially intimidated and frustrated by computers. Although some retirement communities offer computer facilities, technical support may be fragmented or nonexistent. At-home personalized services are a better way for seniors to learn computer skills and become internet-savvy. As part of his concierge services, Dick Padgett of Five Star Concierge helps his clients purchase their computers and peripherals, installs the equipment, and then teaches them how to use it.

Once they are online, seniors generally want to learn about word processing, personal finance, and desktop publishing software. They also enjoy playing computer games and conducting genealogy searches. Make it part of your mission to keep seniors connected through the use of their computers. These services can often include teaching computer basics or more advanced skills, or providing assistance with equipment purchase, software, and equipment upgrades.

Stat Fact

According to the Consumer Expenditure Survey conducted by the Census Bureau, seniors are outspending Generation Xers with online purchases of computer software and hardware, books, music, and clothing. Today's seniors have more time and money to splurge, and they are doing it as gleefully as any mouse potato.

▲

Learn more about starting a computer training business for seniors in Entrepreneur's *Start Your Own E-Learning Business*.

Handyman Business

Have you always been a whiz at fixing things around your own home and dreamed of putting those skills to work as a small-business owner? Minor repairs and maintenance can add up to a major opportunity for you in the form of a handyman business targeting seniors. More often than not, top contractors are too busy to take on smaller projects, and retirees living on fixed incomes can't afford their rates anyway.

If you don't have the skills to personally perform basic handyman projects, you can still launch a handyman service agency in your community or purchase a franchise. Instead of doing the work yourself, you serve as a project coordinator. You meet with clients, assess their needs, and then provide the labor through your own resources network. You pay the subcontractors, mark up their fees a reasonable amount to compensate for your services, and bill the client.

Handymen can provide a wide range of services to make life easier, safer, and more enjoyable for elderly clients. Consider that as people get older, sometimes

Checking In

For a nominal fee (typically $1 to $5 per check), you can make regular phone calls or send emails to homebound seniors to check on their safety, health, and well-being. Initial discussion of the need for these daily or weekly calls may be initiated by a long-distance relative or the elderly person herself. At a pre-arranged time, you can phone a lonely senior and brighten her day with a friendly "hello," unless a computer-savvy senior prefers to be contacted through email.

Find out ahead of time from the person making the arrangements what you're expected to do in the event you are unable to make contact or you think your client is not well. It may be that you will immediately call a relative and notify them of the situation, or perhaps you will personally check on your client— for an additional fee, of course.

This can be a stand-alone service or merged with other concierge services, especially if a simple checkup phone call turns into a request for a prescription pickup, grocery shopping, or a ride to the doctor's office.

even simple chores like raking leaves or putting up storm windows turn into mission impossible. Or, to accommodate their changing physical needs, your clients may need to make modifications to their homes such as installing grab bars or nonskid strips in the bathroom or on stairs. These are all opportunities for you.

The Importance of Fix-It-Ability

A handyman needs to have "fix-it-ability" and be proficient with basic household tools. According to Padgett, if you are going to do handiwork, you need to be comfortable with and have basic knowledge of all types of tools.

> ### Bright Idea
> Many retirees have two homes they live in at different times of the year, and you could care for their property in their absence. Your service could also include preparing the house for their arrival by making sure everything is in working order, or closing up the house (preparing it to be vacant for an extended time by covering furniture, putting up storm shutters, etc.) for the period they will be gone.

Of course, the specific tools you need will depend on the type of work you specialize in or the project you are working on.

Whenever possible, offer your clients choices. For example, if a client has a leaky faucet, will replacing a washer fix it, or will a new faucet need to be installed? And even if a washer will do the job, give the client the option of a new faucet and let her make the decision.

When you are working on a project at a client's home, take a look around and see what else needs repairing. With the customer's permission, perhaps you can take care of it while you are there. But if you are unable to or if the customer is unwilling to have the repairs done at that time, leave behind a written proposal that can be kept for future reference. This will also give you the opportunity to follow up later and remind the customer that you're available to take care of the matter.

If you are going to get into more advanced repairs such as roof repair, electrical rewiring, or plumbing, you will probably need a special license such as a contractor's license or electrician's certification. For some jobs, building permits may be required. Padgett considers himself more of a "handy-husband." If the project is more extensive than he is comfortable with, he will immediately refer his client to an appropriate qualified professional. He says, "If it sounds like something I don't think I want to touch, I tell people, 'I can look for somebody to do that for you and I will find somebody and I will recommend them to you, but I don't think it is something I'd do myself.' I don't tackle things I don't think I should do." Padgett says it wasn't his original intention to do handyman work as part of his concierge service, but as clients kept asking him if he could fix a doorknob or hang a picture, his business evolved to include that service.

Getting Started

Startup costs are typically low for a handyman business. You will, of course, need general household tools, but you probably already own most of what you will need. You'll also need transportation. Although you don't need to have a truck or van, those are usually the preferred vehicles because they are roomier and can carry more equipment.

In most areas of the country, you will need a business license. Check with the state and local jurisdictions to see what is required for this type of trade. Also talk to your insurance agent about what type of liability coverage and bonding you will need.

What to Charge

Wondering what to charge? It really depends on where you are, so you'll need to do some homework. Many seniors live on fixed incomes and count every nickel; others have greater financial resources but are products of the Depression years and choose to live frugally; still others will pay any price. Determine a competitive rate that will cover overhead and allow an adequate profit that is at the same time reasonable and affordable to your customers.

You can price each job individually or bill an hourly rate. In Orlando, Florida, the hourly rate is about $35, plus materials. By contrast, Padgett in San Diego charges an hourly fee of $46. In other parts of the country, such as Denver, a handyman's fee averages $75 to $100 an hour.

Depending on the size of the job and how long it's going to take to complete, you may ask for a small deposit to cover your out-of-pocket costs. If supplies or parts are going to be substantial, you may ask customers to purchase those items themselves or pay you in advance for that portion of the project, and then bill your labor when everything is finished.

If you need special tools for particular jobs, buy them as needed. There may be times when you can bill the client for the tool.

Check with your local home and building supply stores to see what benefits or discounts they offer commercial customers. For example, Lowe's Home Improvement (www.lowes.com) and Home Depot (www.homedepot.com) have business accounts with revolving commercial credit for small- to medium-sized operations. Ace Hardware (www.acehardware.com) has a Helpful

Bright Idea

Set up a system that helps keep the work flowing and the deadlines met. Some operators create a computerized spreadsheet; others simply mark their work on a project board or calendar. The key is to come up with a system that works for you so you won't overcommit yourself.

Hardware Club that features special discounts, coupons, and a free subscription to its *Homeplace* magazine. All three websites feature a variety of helpful articles.

Is This an Emergency?

Set guidelines for how quickly you will be able to respond to customer calls. Phone calls should be returned the same day, and you may want to commit to being on the job site to provide an estimate within 24 to 48 hours of the initial call.

Decide if you are going to offer an expedited response for emergencies, and set parameters for that. You may promise a returned phone call within two hours and being on site within six hours, regardless of the time or day. Fees for expedited services will naturally be higher than for regular service.

Presenting Yourself

For everyone's protection, provide a written estimate or agreement that is signed by both the customer and you. Consider offering a guarantee of 6 to 12 months on labor (parts would be covered by the manufacturer's warranty). For instance, let's say you installed a doorknob, and it starts to loosen in a month or so. Let your client know you'll come back and tighten it at no charge—as long as the product is not defective.

In addition to doing a good job for a reasonable fee, you should look presentable. You don't have to dress up, but you should at least wear a clean shirt and keep it tucked in. For a more professional appearance, wear a shirt with your company's logo and your first name on it.

And speaking of logos, if you can't afford or don't want to have a logo painted on your vehicle, use magnetic signs instead. This type of traveling billboard can generate business as you cruise around town.

Staffing

When the time comes, you'll need reliable people with varied skills to provide the specific services your clients need. The exact positions you'll want to fill will depend on the nature and scope of your particular operation. Consider how you will handle staffing as you grow, and address that in your business plan—but remain flexible and ready to make changes in your strategy if your market requires it. Especially in the startup phase, you'll find it a challenge to achieve the perfect balance between staffing resources and client needs. Once your business is established, it will get easier.

The mechanics of staffing—including finding, screening, and hiring employees; benefits; salary ranges; and other personnel issues—are discussed in Chapter 12.

8

Transportation
Service

Transportation is a major obstacle for many seniors who are trying to remain independent and self-sufficient. Some seniors prefer to let others drive, even though they may still have a car and a license; others wisely turn in their keys when they are unable to drive safely; still others may find themselves faced with a situation that temporarily prevents them from driving.

Nondriving seniors often rely on family members or neighbors for transportation, but these resources may not always be available. Many community transportation systems, such as public and paratransit (specialized transportation service for persons who are unable to use regular public transportation due to a disability or health-related condition), are not considered senior-friendly because many seniors can't walk to a bus stop, can't easily get into or out of a van, or can't afford a taxi.

Doug Iannelli, owner of Appointment Companions in Atlanta, Georgia, not only transports clients to and from their appointments, he also stays with them throughout the duration to offer assistance and companionship. "I'm their eyes and ears," Iannelli says. "I can also be in contact with family members if the senior chooses so that while they are in the doctor's office they can have direct contact."

Seniors need this type of reliable, comfortable transportation with sensitive, responsible drivers who will wait for them at the doctor's office, escort them when shopping and running errands, and most important, be where they are supposed to be on time so the client is not left waiting.

Defining Your Service

One of the first decisions you need to make is how specialized your senior transportation service will be. Will you target able-bodied elderly folks who want to go on errands, shopping expeditions, and other outings? Will you operate vehicles that can accommodate wheelchairs and walkers by installing lifts, ramps, and/or security restraints necessary for these mobility devices? Or will you serve seniors with even greater disabilities? For example, an elderly person may be mentally impaired, have cerebral palsy, use an oxygen tank, or have a hearing or vision disability that may require the use of a service animal.

Dick Padgett, owner of Five Star Concierge in San Diego, transports seniors with wheelchairs and walkers, but he does not have special equipment on his van. His clients are able to get in and out of their wheelchairs with his assistance; if they were not, he would refer them to a transportation service that had a wheelchair ramp or lift.

Iannelli also uses a traditional mini-van for his transportation service, but contracts with a wheelchair transport company when needed.

> **Tip...**
>
> **Smart Tip**
> General Motors offers financial assistance to customers installing eligible mobility equipment, such as wheelchair lifts, ramps, and automatic door openers. For information on current programs, call (800) 323-9935 or visit the website at www.gmmobility.com/mobility-financial-assistance/.

"In a situation like that I will meet the client at their residence and accompany them in the van so that I can help them to and from their appointment," he says.

If you decide to transport those who cannot get into or out of their wheelchairs, you will need a midsized or larger van that is equipped with a wheelchair lift and four-point tie-downs or restraints to secure the wheelchairs. In addition, you will also need safety restraints for unoccupied wheelchairs and/or walkers.

You can buy a new or used van with a wheelchair lift already installed, or have the lift installed at a later time. Ask your dealer which lift works best with that specific vehicle. Shop carefully for the best prices, warranties, and service offers for ramps and lifts. In addition to shopping local dealers, be sure to check the internet for deals on lifts.

Regulatory Issues

Check with your state Department of Transportation to see what regulations will apply to your business. Be very clear about the specifics of your operation because many states do not have legislation or restrictions for this type of service, and you want to avoid undue regulatory burdens.

When you are moving people around via public roads for compensation, the rules and regulations vary not only state-to-state, but also town-to-town. Check with all the jurisdictions in which you plan to operate to see what they require. For instance, some states do not require a special license for a transportation business, but counties within those states do. To be safe, follow the most stringent guidelines that are set out by all the jurisdictions and obtain all the required permits and licenses.

Iannelli says that it's important to talk to your insurance agent in detail before you start driving people around for money. Even if you are using your personal vehicle, you will probably need to get commercial insurance. And some states, such as California, have a Public Utilities Commission (PUC) that requires driver drug testing and additional insurance for a transportation service. Padgett's insurance agent contacted the PUC on his behalf. "They agreed that I was an exception [to commercial automobile use restrictions] and didn't need a PUC license because I charged strictly for my time and not by the mile," he says. "So I just needed commercial liability car insurance."

> **Tip...**
>
> ## Smart Tip
> Check with *Consumer Reports* at consumer reports.org to find out what vehicles are recommended for your transportation needs. For a small subscription fee, you will have access to ratings for thousands of products related to your home or business.

▲

Staffing

A transportation service can easily be started as a one-person operation, but as you grow you may find the need to hire additional drivers. In the following sections, we outline policies and procedures, as well as offer some guidelines to help you with the process of hiring dependable drivers for your business. You may also need to find reliable employees to answer phones, schedule transportation for clients, and other administrative tasks. In Chapter 12, we discuss the mechanics of staffing—including finding, screening, and hiring employees; benefits; salary ranges; and other personnel issues. How you will handle staffing in your company should be addressed in detail in your business plan.

Spell It Out

Create a detailed policies and procedures document that addresses every aspect of your operation, from the services you provide, to drivers you hire, to what you expect from your clients. Issues your policy should address include:

- *Driver's license*. All drivers must have a driver's license that is valid in the state in which you are operating; some states may also require a commercial license.
- *Registration*. A copy of the vehicle's registration must remain in the vehicle at all times. A copy of the insurance card or certificate should also be kept with the registration.
- *Passenger checklist*. Each driver should be provided with a sheet that identifies his or her passengers, emergency contact information, and special needs in the event of an injury or illness.
- *Smoking*. Smoking should be prohibited in any vehicles used to transport seniors, even if it's the driver's own personal vehicle. In the case of a personal vehicle, even if the driver doesn't smoke while clients are in the car but does on other occasions, the smell may be offensive.
- *Intoxicating substances*. A driver should not have consumed any alcohol for at least 12 hours prior to operating a vehicle that transports seniors. Make it clear that the use of illegal drugs is strictly prohibited, and establish a mandatory drug testing policy. Drivers should also be required to report if they are taking prescribed or over-the-counter medications that could impair their abilities in any way.

> **Bright Idea**
> In lieu of charging mileage, consider invoicing fees at an hourly rate billed in 15-minute increments that will cover your time regardless of whether you are driving, shopping, or waiting for your client.

- *Music.* Do not play music or the radio in the vehicle. Many seniors have hearing disabilities, and the added noise may confuse or disorient them. Drivers should not wear headphones while operating the vehicle.

- *Seat belts.* Seat belts and safety restraints must be used by all drivers and passengers at all times—no exceptions.

- *Internal environment.* Keep the internal vehicle temperature comfortable by air-conditioning if the outside temperature rises above 75 degrees, or by turning on the heat if it drops below 60 degrees. Some people don't like wind blowing on them, so instead of opening windows, it may be prudent to run the air conditioning all the time at a comfortable temperature (except when heat is needed).

- *Passenger supervision.* Never leave your passenger(s) unsupervised for any length of time. When you arrive at a destination, be sure a caregiver or other responsible adult is on the premises so that the client will not be left alone.

- *Communications.* Provide each driver with a cell phone or two-way handheld radio to use in the event of emergencies, to find directions, or to report any problems regarding the pickup or drop-off of a client.

- *First-aid kit.* Keep a first-aid kit in any vehicle that is used to transport seniors, as well as a road emergency kit. In addition, have a bottle of drinking water, blanket, hand sanitizer or wipes, and spare change (for tolls or pay telephones) on hand at all times.

- *Uniforms.* Your drivers should wear uniforms or at least matching polo shirts with your business logo on the front. This allows the driver to be easily identified and creates a more professional image for your company.

- *Driving techniques.* When operating the vehicle, drivers should always accelerate, stop, and turn slowly and smoothly to assure the comfort of their passengers.

Designated Drivers

Candidates for driving positions with your senior transportation service should complete an application form that will give you sufficient information to thoroughly investigate their backgrounds. Be sure to check their automobile insurance and motor vehicle records, and kick them to the curb if they have had any traffic violations, at-fault accidents, or criminal activity within the past three years.

In addition to clean driving records, your drivers should have training in CPR, first aid, and how to properly use any special equipment, such as a wheelchair lift if your vehicle has one. You should also require that they complete a defensive driving course; this will not only protect your clients, but it may also reduce your insurance rates.

In the people-moving business, drivers need more than just technical skill. Hire people who are pleasant, patient, and sensitive to their passengers. Drivers need to

By the Numbers

Three national surveys were conducted to identify Supplemental Transportation Programs for seniors throughout the United States. According to the Beverly Foundation (a nonprofit organization whose mission is to enhance the health and well-being of older adults) in Pasadena, California, and the Washington, DC-based AAA Foundation for Traffic Safety (a public charity dedicated to identifying traffic safety problems and researching possible solutions), these surveys provide information on how senior transportation programs are organized, how they are funded, what they do, whom they serve, and how they operate.

- *Where are they?* Forty percent target rural areas, 21 percent are in urban areas, 13 percent are in the suburbs, and 28 percent are in mixed areas.
- *How long have they been in business?* Fifty percent have been established since the mid-1980s.
- *How are they organized?* Eighty percent are nonprofit.
- *What is their purpose?* Sixty-one percent are for medical appointments, 42 percent are for social activities, 19 percent are for religious functions, and 35 percent are for any purpose.
- *What type of services do they provide?* Seventy-one percent offer door-to-door service (drivers escort and assist passengers from the door of departure to the door of their destination), 19 percent have curb-to-curb service (drivers pick up and take passengers as close to the door as possible, but generally do not provide assistance getting on and off the bus or van), and 10 percent are on a fixed route (e.g., bus route).
- *Will they escort seniors?* Forty-seven percent do so.
- *What type of vehicles do they use?* Forty-two percent use automobiles, 50 percent use vans, 29 percent use buses, and 6 percent use taxis.
- *How do they charge?* Fifty-seven percent do not charge fees, 21 percent use a flat-rate fee, 11 percent charge by mileage, and 8 percent use a sliding fee.
- *Who are their drivers?* Thirty-four percent are volunteers, 42 percent are paid drivers, and 20 percent are a mix of volunteers and paid drivers.
- *How are they funded?* Sixty-three percent receive grants, 51 percent charge fees or receive donations from riders, and 18 percent are funded through tax revenue.
- *In what areas do they report having problems?* Forty-one percent report finances are problematic, 36 percent say that driver issues are a problem, and 40percent maintain that insurance is a challenge.

exhibit understanding and compassion for your clients, treating them with dignity and respect. Some seniors may need assistance getting in and out of the vehicle, and others may become confused or upset—often for no apparent reason—so it's important for the driver to be patient and willing to lend a helping hand when needed.

> **Tip...**
>
> **Smart Tip**
> Choose safe vehicles. They don't have to be fresh off the dealer's lot, but ideally they should have fewer than 50,000 miles on the odometer and not be more than four years old. These vehicles should always be properly inspected and regularly maintained.

Padgett feels that providing transportation for seniors is more than just being a driver; it's also being a friend. Seniors make up a big part of his concierge transportation business. He says, "When I drive them to the doctor, some of them get a little confused, so I actually go inside with them and wait. Some have even asked me to come into the exam room with them and write down what the doctor says, because they can't always remember." Even when he drops clients off at a senior day care, he walks them inside and personally turns them over to the caregiver. Sometimes he will have a disoriented senior tell him where they want to go, which is different than where he knows he is supposed to take them. "So I kind of talk to them like I'm doing what they want, even though I'm not," he says.

You will also want to consider if the driver can handle all the senior passengers on board, or if an additional person may need to ride along. If so, this person should also be properly trained as a driver.

What to Charge

Decide if you want to charge a flat fee from point to point or a per-mile rate. Or you can combine the two fee structures by establishing a minimum plus a per-mile charge; for example, charge a $50 minimum that includes the first 10 miles, and $6.00 a mile thereafter. For regular customers who travel the same routes, you may establish a weekly fare.

Your fee needs to cover your expenses and allow for a profit. Consider the price of having a vehicle in service (the cost of the vehicle amortized over its expected service life, repairs and maintenance, fuel, insurance), labor, and overhead, and then add 15 to 20 percent for your profit. Use the Vehicle Cost Worksheet on page 102 to figure your costs.

Think about how many passengers you can transport and the type of services they will need: one-way, round trip, or special trip, and include whether your vehicle has been equipped to meet special needs, such as having a wheelchair lift. This will help you determine a fair and reasonable rate that you can charge your riders.

Vehicle Cost Worksheet

Note: This example is based on a previously owned 15-passenger van purchased for $20,000 (including finance charges) that you anticipate using for the next five years.

Straight amortization	$4,000
Insurance	$2,000
License, fees, and taxes	$500
Fuel cost	$2,490
Flexible expenses (overhead)	$1,250
Maintenance and repairs	$500
Labor (part-time driver)	$10,000
Tolls and parking fees	$900
Subtotal annual cost	$21,640
Plus 15 percent profit margin	$3,246
Total annual cost	**$24,886**

Divide the total annual cost figure by an estimated annual mileage of 18,250 (an estimate of the average mileage for a one-vehicle transportation service in most cities) to determine what your cost per mile is, which in this case is approximately $1.36. In this scenario, if you transport an average of 20 people a week at $30 each or $2.50 per mile, you will surpass your targeted profit margin.

These are only estimated expenses, and you will need to insert your own figures. Naturally, your annual mileage will be contingent on your geographical location. If you live in a densely populated city, you may not drive your client more than 5 to 10 miles one way. On the other hand, if you live in a more rural area, you may drive a round trip of 40 to 50 miles. In the startup stage, you'll have to estimate many of these amounts using a "best guess" strategy. After you've been in operation for a while, you'll have real numbers to use as a basis, and you can make adjustments as necessary in your rate structure.

Consider including a fuel surcharge in your contract so that your profits won't be eaten away when gas prices go up. The best way to do this is to insert a clause that will allow you to raise the fees by a certain percentage if the cost of gasoline exceeds a specific amount.

Equipping Your Business

Startup costs for a transportation business with a homebased location and one vehicle in the beginning can be as low as a few thousand dollars. You don't need a lot of equipment to get your senior transportation business started. Your biggest expense will be a reliable vehicle, which could be a minivan or 15-passenger van. Other considerations are whether or not to provide mobility equipment, such as a wheelchair lift or ramp. You will also need adequate commercial car insurance.

In addition to basic office equipment (see Chapter 13), you'll need a few specialized pieces of equipment in this business. Use the Transportation Service Equipment Checklist below to make sure you haven't forgotten anything.

As your business grows, you may want to invest in additional vehicles, as well as lease or purchase a commercial facility in which to park the vehicles. In that event, you will need from $25,000 to $150,000 to properly equip your transportation business.

Transportation Service Equipment Checklist

❏ Mini or passenger van (new)	$20,000–$42,000
❏ Mini or passenger van (used—4 years old)	$11,000–$22,000
❏ Wheelchair lift	$1,000–$3,300
❏ Wheelchair ramp	$260–$2,300
❏ 1 Set of wheelchair safety restraints or tie-downs	$200–$460
❏ Cell phone	$99–$599
❏ Two-way handheld radio	$150–$300
❏ First-aid kit	$15–$150

Travel
Service

Today's seniors have better health, wealth, and education, along with more time on their hands, than previous generations. They have become the leading influence in the travel industry, and marketers are paying closer attention. Demographic trends are clear. According to statistics provided by the Travel Industry Association of America, the mature market

(55+) will gain in travel intensity over the next 20 years. Anticipated long-term trends are an increase in adult-only travel parties, a decline in travelers looking for "traditional" family experiences, more "soft adventure" tours for outdoor activities, and an increased interest in local heritage and culture. Senior travelers are becoming more independent, preferring less group travel. However, they still want well-organized agendas and prearranged transportation.

In this chapter, we focus on the special travel needs of seniors, whether it's accommodating physical limitations, offering opportunities for companionship, or planning specialty tours. This particular niche represents a tremendous opportunity for travel agents and tour operators who want to target the senior market.

Travel Investment

Statistics from the U.S. Bureau of Labor Statistics indicate that the amount of money spent on travel will rise significantly over the next decade. Worldwide, travel and tourism is an $8 trillion business, and in ten years that number will reach $15 trillion, according to the World Travel & Tourism Council (WTTC). The WTTC's long-term forecasts point to steady growth for world travel and tourism averaging 4.4 percent a year between now and 2018. Younger people and families might splurge on vacations, but the senior population considers these expeditions an investment. It's true that seniors have more disposable income in the bank than ever before, but they are looking for value and usually aren't frivolous with their savings.

Many seniors are traveling on funds from their 401(k)s, IRAs, or other retirement accounts. People look at their vacations and say to themselves, "OK, now I'm making an investment. How am I going to get the most out of it?" So they will ask a lot of questions to make sure they are getting the best return on their money. For these folks it's not just taking the funds out of a paycheck; they are taking them out of their retirement.

Stat Fact
In a recent survey by the Travel Industry Association of America and Smithsonian magazine, 81 percent of travelers reported including cultural, arts, and heritage activities in their trips.

What's Your Specialty?

The travel industry is probably more diverse than most. Because there is an amazing amount of ground to cover, this book is not going to attempt to cover it. However, it is going to focus on a few areas that seem to be of significant interest to many senior travelers, and hopefully to you.

When clients contact you, they are not only asking you to find the best options and the best prices, but they are also counting on your guidance. Your insight and the ability to make good recommendations based on your clients' needs and preferences will be your most valuable asset. You cannot be an expert in every area of the travel industry; it's too vast. But if you narrow your niche to a targeted market, such as disabled travelers, travel companions, cruises for women, etc., you will become known as an expert in that field, and your business will prosper. Anya Clowers of Jet With Comfort decided to focus on niche travel groups such as seniors. "I wanted to help senior travelers identify their needs before they planned travel," she says. "With the tools, tips, and services I recommend, I prepare them to travel self-sufficiently no matter what the situation."

Specific Age Groups

When defining your target market, you may want to narrow your focus to a specific age group, such as older baby boomers (55 to 64), retirees (65 to 75), or the very mature (75-plus). Each group has different dynamics and needs. By becoming a specialist in that market, your business can expand to meet the travel needs of that age group.

The very mature senior traveler is more likely to observe from afar. For them, their vacation is a way to relax, have some companionship, eat well, and enjoy good shows. On the other hand, retired baby boomers basically want to touch and feel. They don't want to just visit a port town; they might want to canoe in that area, do a little fishing, or play golf. They are more interested in being actively involved.

Stat Fact

The Bureau of Labor Statistics reports that the median annual earnings for travel agents in 2010 were $31,870, with the top 10 percent earning more than $50,620. Self-employed agents often achieve smaller earnings as they are getting established, but stand to earn upward of six figures at the upper end of the scale, particularly those who cater to high-end luxury travelers.

Luxury Travel

Luxury traveling caters to a posh demographic and you will not have any competition from the thousands of discount travel agencies. Affluent customers are willing to spend more to get more, which means a luxury travel specialist will need to resonate with people who consider exotic travel to be a lifestyle. Like any other specialty area you should be familiar with your targeted market to make a lasting impression by providing travel experiences that are unique, vibrant, and supremely comfortable. The well-to-do senior enjoys five-star resorts in trendy destinations, along with experiencing native cuisine and local attractions. They also place considerable importance on personalized service and attention to details.

Many upscale senior travelers are retaining agents who act as "travel concierges," by planning exclusive, custom-made travel packages and taking their clients to popular destinations around the world—in style. This includes making all the arrangements from travel and lodging to dinner reservations and theater tickets.

Soft-Adventure Tours

Adventure means different things to different people. For some it might be going to Tanzania for a wildlife safari; others might get a thrill from windjamming in the Caribbean. Soft-adventure tours are vacations designed for the active 50-plus traveler. This style of travel has been one of the fastest-growing segments of the senior tour industry for more than ten years. It generally includes basic accommodations, along with walking, hiking, or bicycling over terrain that is often rough and uneven. These expeditions are not recommended for people with physical limitations or disabilities, although the pace is toned down from the more energetic adventure tours designed for younger people.

Bear in mind that if you're not an expert in a particular outdoor or adventure field, you're not going to have much success. For example, you certainly don't want to attempt navigating the Amazon in a small riverboat if you've never done it before.

Grandtravel

Grandparents today are not like the grandparents of yesterday; greater numbers are more energetic, active, and adventurous. They don't want to stay home and look after the grandkids. Instead, they want to pack their grandchildren up and take them along on fun-filled vacations, while leaving the parents at home to take a breather. As an added bonus, most of the time senior and children's discounts can be factored into the package for added savings.

Grandtravel is a specialized niche that is becoming one of the fastest-growing travel trends, representing more than 21 percent of all trips taken with children last year, according to the Travel Industry Association of America. Because geographical distances separate many families, special trips bring grandparents and grandchildren together to strengthen bonds and create lasting memories.

Travel agencies and resorts are picking up on the trend and designing packages that combine

> **Smart Tip**
>
> Tip...
>
> Be sure your clients know whether taxes and gratuities are included in their fares. Also make it clear what transportation, meals, and entertainment are included in their packages and what will have to be paid for separately.

recreational, educational and cultural trips for grandparents and grandchildren to enjoy together. For example, the Loews hotel chain has created "Generation G" programs designed for grandparents vacationing with their grandchildren that feature fun and educational activities.

For Women Only

Recently, *Road and Travel* magazine reported that women influence 85 percent of all travel decisions. According to the most recent statistics provided by the U.S. Census Bureau, mature women outnumber mature men by a ratio of 100 to 81 (age 55 to 64), 100 to 82 (age 65 to 74), 100 to 69 (age 75 to 84), and 100 to 49 (age 85-plus). Older women travelers are predicted by the Travel Industry Association of America to be one of the driving forces behind senior travel in the long term. Although spas and cruises remain popular choices for women, dozens of other special interest trips are springing up like wine-tasting in Napa Valley, making handicrafts with the locals in Costa Rica, or shopping in Versailles.

For both safety and companionship, many women prefer to travel in small groups instead of alone. Cruises remain a popular choice for single women; some cruise lines offer a "Gentleman Hosts" program where carefully screened senior gentlemen volunteer to serve as dance partners during onboard social functions.

Although women have made great strides over the generations, they are still at their most vulnerable when traveling—especially when cultural differences are involved. In addition to secure and reliable travel arrangements, good tour operators advise their clients on the laws and customs of specific countries. This is especially important when Westerners are visiting areas such as the Middle East, where customs can be significantly different, and women in particular may need to make special accommodations in how they dress and act in public.

Cruising Along

Cruises are one of the hottest segments of the travel industry that is steadily growing as new and exciting excursions are departing from a wide range of ports. In addition to a fun variety of dining opportunities, spacious suites, and top-rate entertainment, cruises also provide the opportunity to visit exotic locales around the world.

The older population is the mainstay of the cruise industry, as statistics indicate that almost 70 percent of passengers are seniors. To accommodate the more refined tastes of their elder customers, cruise ships offer activities such as ballroom dancing, wine tasting, and shore excursions that highlight cultural and historic places of interest. Their port destinations are longer treks to exotic regions like Scandinavia, the South Pacific, and the Mediterranean.

Beware!
Not everything that glitters is gold—just because a senior discount is offered doesn't mean it's a better deal. Carefully compare senior discount offers, especially airfare. You may find that a regular fare is a better bargain. There may also be severe restrictions placed on the discounted fares that may be too difficult for the client.

Most major cruise ships have a staffed medical facility to handle emergencies, which a travel agent will need to confirm. However, if your client has a medical condition, check with the cruise line to make sure it will be able to handle any specific needs, if necessary.

Senior Travelers with Disabilities

Older travelers with disabilities have more opportunities than ever to explore the world with the assistance of high-tech support and creative planning. Relaxing "dialysis cruises" using portable dialysis equipment have been designed for travelers who have such special medical needs; fun and exciting road trips are taken by senior adults and their families in vans and buses that are wheelchair-accessible and can transport portable nebulizers and oxygen cylinders; customized tours and travel packages are frequently put together for visually or hearing-impaired customers. These trips can often accommodate service animals.

When planning a tour for seniors who have physical limitations, consider the accessibility of the facilities on your itinerary. Are there steps that will need to be navigated? Even one step could be a problem for someone in a wheelchair or using a walker. Does the museum have elevators large enough to accommodate wheelchairs? Are the restrooms in the basilica handicapped-accessible? Are aisles and walkways at the quaint little antique village wide enough for wheelchairs and scooters? Are the sidewalks in the town rough and uneven?

As each country has its own standards, disabled clients traveling abroad may face additional challenges regarding transportation and accessibility. Advance research and planning are a necessity so your clients can have a safe and enjoyable trip. Provide international travelers with disabilities copies of the pamphlets, *New Horizons: Information for the Air Traveler with a Disability*, that can be ordered from the Department of Transportation by calling (202) 366-4000 or visiting www.dot.gov.

Make sure disabled clients know their rights when traveling and know what to do if they encounter discrimination. Contact the Department of Transportation for a list of the steps taken by the U.S. government to ensure the civil rights of people with disabilities when traveling by air, ground, or water. This information also covers the use of service animals.

European countries do not have the same regulations that the United States has for disabled travelers. Some countries will make every effort to provide accessibility

Stat Fact

A study done by the Open Doors Organization—a nonprofit disability education organization—the Travel Industry Association of America, and the Society for Accessible Transportation and Hospitality found that disabled travelers spend approximately $3.3 billion a year on travel. However, if the travel industry properly accommodated them, that figure could rise to more than $27 billion per year.

for handicapped travelers, while others do not have the resources or same concerns about disabled persons. Before recommending a tour or putting together a trip package, carefully research accessibility concerns for transportation, hotel accommodations, dining, and sightseeing.

For travelers with disabilities, Moss Rehabilitation Hospital in Philadelphia sponsors a free Travel Information Service to assist with planning trips domestically and abroad. Go to mossresourcenet.org or see the "Miscellaneous Resources" section in the Appendix for contact information.

The Society for Accessible Transportation and Hospitality works to promote awareness, respect, and accessibility for disabled and older travelers. It is part of the organization's mission to educate the travel, tourism, and hospitality industry about being more accessible for persons with disabilities in accordance with the Americans with Disabilities Act of 1990 and the Air Carriers Access Act. For more information, visit www.sath.org.

Travel Partners or Companions

Travel companions have been used for centuries to ensure safety, share adventures, and offer companionship. They provide camaraderie while dining and sightseeing, keep an eye on the luggage while the client visits the restroom or makes a phone call, and help to discourage pickpockets and scam artists. Often health-care professionals will offer their services as travel partners to accompany elderly clients who may need additional medical attention while on vacation.

Doug Iannelli started his Flying Companions business to assist seniors and disabled passengers fly anywhere in the world. "We actually travel with the senior from airport to airport and handle all of the flight logistics and trip details so they have a relaxed flying experience," he says. This includes coordinating all of the flight arrangements, wheelchair assistance, check-in, luggage help, carry-ons, and navigating security.

Iannelli says he learned from experience to fly to the destination the day before he plans on meeting his client. This way, if there is an unforeseen weather delay or aircraft mechanical delay, he is still able to greet the client in time for their flight the following day. "On my second trip with a client, I decided to take a connecting flight the morning of our trip," Iannelli relates. "I missed the connection and had to push both the client's and my flight back. This mishap cost me a lot of money to change our itinerary. Needless to say, that is why I fly in the day before our arranged flight."

Fees for travel companions vary because so many factors are involved. For example, would this be a one-way or round trip flight? Does the client need assistance for the entire trip or just airport to airport? In addition to accompanying the senior client, travel companions generally help facilitate travel arrangements, such as making reservations, planning an itinerary, and arranging transportation.

Shopping Expeditions

Everyone loves a great bargain, especially ardent shoppers who can turn a shopping spree into the ultimate challenge. According to the Travel Industry Association, approximately 55 million people plan trips around outlet-mall shopping each year. But why stop at the mall? Pre-planned shopping missions can be anywhere from a day trip to San Francisco's Chinatown to a weekend jaunt in the Amish Country to a fortnight browsing for antiques in Brussels.

Historical Jaunts

In a recent survey by the Travel Industry Association and *Smithsonian* magazine, 81 percent of travelers reported including cultural, arts, and heritage activities in their trips. This was confirmed when last year more than 53 million tourists pursued historic and cultural interests. These included museums, galleries, battlefields, cities, and other sites. As a tour operator, you can plan historical vacations to see the Roman ruins in Tunisia or visit Renaissance festivals in the Carolinas. The possibilities are endless, as well as educational and fun!

Group Packages

Andi McClure-Mysza, President of the Independent Contractor Division for Montrose Travel (montrosetravel.com), feels that group travel is probably one of the most profitable ways a travel agent or tour operator can run their business. She recommends targeting specific markets for advertising purposes. "Perhaps

Bright Idea

For more information on how to learn more about the nuts and bolts of starting a travel and tours business, including finding host agencies and specialty travel carriers see Entrepreneur's startup guide, *Start Your Own Travel Business and More* written by Rich Mintzer. Another good resource for starting a travel business is *Design and Launch an Online Travel Business in a Week* by Charlene Davis, which is part of Entrepreneur's new *Click Start* series.

International Travel Health Concerns

Address health issues for your senior travel clients in advance. The Centers for Disease Control and Prevention (CDC) publishes an annual booklet titled *Health Information for International Travel* (also referred to as the Yellow Book). It includes immunization advice, details of disease, health risks for specific countries, and information on how travelers can stay healthy. To obtain a copy of this booklet, call (800) 451-7556 or go to www.nc.cdc.gov/travel/yellowbook/.

International travelers should also contact their local health department at least four weeks before departing for a foreign country to obtain current information about health issues at their destinations. In addition, the Centers for Disease Control and Prevention has a 24-hour automated international traveler's hotline at (404) 332-4559 and a website at cdc.gov.

The International Association for Medical Assistance to Travelers provides information about vaccination requirements, health risks, and sanitary, climatic, and environmental conditions around the world. For information, visit iamat.org or call (716) 754-4883.

you want to promote a group cruise that's all about health and fitness," she says. "Sign up the personal trainer at a local gym to be the featured speaker and guest on the ship. Then ask the gym to give you their mailing list or let you piggyback on a mailing they are already sending out." Not only do you have 50 people signed up for the health and fitness cruise, but you have 50 potential customers who might be taking their own vacations in the near future.

Getting Started

The most important qualification for becoming an independent travel agent who specializes in senior travel is enjoying travel yourself. When you are enthusiastic and knowledgeable, you'll make powerful and inspiring sales presentations. Plus you'll enjoy the fringe benefits that come in the form of travel discounts and freebies that you'll receive as you plan itineraries for others.

Smart Tip
The U.S. Department of State has a wealth of information for domestic and international travelers. A special tip sheet for older Americans can be found at travel.state.gov.

Most states do not require testing or licensing for travel agents, although you may need to register with your state's Department of Revenue to collect and remit certain taxes. Check with your state's business licensing or professional regulation department to determine the specific requirements for your operation. You may also need a local occupational license (see Chapter 10 for details).

Although you don't have to be certified as a travel agent to operate as one, you'll have more credibility with your clients if you take courses and become credentialed in your specialty area. Many of these courses are offered online and are inexpensive. Check to see if there are any travel schools or vocational schools offering travel courses in your area. Some colleges and universities also offer courses in travel and tourism.

One way to get started is to work with an existing local agency that serves your niche, such as grandtravel or senior casino cruises. You agree to refer clients, and you earn a commission for every trip booked. Once you have built an established clientele, you'll be ready to open your own operation. Be sure to clearly spell out the details of your agreement with the agency, particularly when it comes to issues such as noncompete requirements. This type of independent travel agent is sometimes called a "referral agent," and that person does exactly as the name implies: refers clients to travel agencies, who in turn pay the agent a small commission. This is probably the easiest way to break into the travel agent business—but it is also the least lucrative.

Working with a Host Agency

As a travel specialist, you can sell airline tickets if that is part of your business plan; however, you may not actually write them unless you are already a brick-and-mortar travel agency looking to expand your business online. To write tickets you need to have an appointment from the Airlines Reporting Corporation (ARC), and they do not grant appointments (which are like licenses) to an agency that is not housed in a commercial office space.

So how do you sell airline tickets? Most homebased travel agents affiliate themselves with a host agency, which is a commercially-based outfit with an ARC appointment. The travel specialist is an independent contractor—sort of a freelance salesperson— finding and maintaining his or her own clients, selling travel products to them, and then splitting commissions with the host agency. When clients need airline tickets, the agent makes the arrangements but has the host agency do the actual ticket printing.

This is a terrific relationship that works well for everyone involved. The travel professional doesn't need to worry about that elusive ARC appointment, and the host agency gets additional profit with a minimum of extra work.

The real reason this relationship is a winner is there are so many more products that can be sold than airline tickets, and these products pay much higher commissions.

Tours and cruises of all sorts abound, and the companies that provide them pay commissions of ten percent or more. Since many of these products are priced much higher than airline tickets, selling them is a lot more lucrative than selling seats on planes.

Montrose Travel (montrosetravel.com) is a family owned and operated travel agency that also operates as a host (mtravel.com) for homebased travel agents, with more than 320 travel professionals under their umbrella. "An individual could technically join us

How to Choose a Host Agency

Rich Mintzer, author of *Start Your Own Travel Business and More* (Entrepreneur Press) offers these tips on how to choose a good host agency:

One of the best things you can do is talk to other agents who work with a host agency and find out if it is paying its commissions on time and giving the support that the agents need.

The goal is to find a host agency that is not a card mill, but will provide you with the travel suppliers and support you need. Mainstream hosts belong to organizations like the Outside Sales Support Network (OSSN) and National Association of Commissioned Travel Agents (NACTA); card mill people don't because they aren't welcome. To find a list of legitimate host agencies, visit the Professional Association of Travel Hosts, Inc. (PATH) at pathonline.travel.

You also want to find out:

- ○ how long a host agency has been in business
- ○ if it is properly licensed and bonded
- ○ what kind of support and/or training it offers
- ○ what its commission breakdown is (and if there are any deductions)
- ○ what associations it is affiliated with (ARC, CLIA, etc.)
- ○ how many travel suppliers and preferred suppliers it works with
- ○ what fees it charges and how often it charges
- ○ how will it communicate with you

Also make sure it has emergency support and is up-to-date on the latest in technology. PATH also suggests that you check to see if it has $1 million in E&O insurance.

today and call themselves a travel agent tomorrow," says Andi McClure-Mysza, president of the Independent Contractor Division for Montrose Travel. "Of course they have to pass the criminal background check first. And we want to make sure they are serious about running a travel business and not just looking for personal discounts."

Like most host agencies, Montrose provides its agents with many services, including ongoing training, accounting, and technology support, errors and omissions insurance, access to the Global Distribution System (GDS), and the ability to issue tickets through ARC. Members are also provided with a professionally designed website that has online booking capabilities—a huge perk for customers who want to handle their own travel arrangements.

"We want our agents to succeed, so we're going to provide them with all of the tools they need," says McClure-Mysza. "We don't make money unless our agents are making money, so our interests are completely aligned."

McClure-Mysza recommends that anyone interested in getting into this part of the travel industry to sign up with a host until they are bringing in $1 million to $2 million dollars annually. "There's a whole sub-industry now with host agencies that allows people to establish themselves in a creditable, reputable way."

Of course, you don't have to work with an accredited host agency to provide your clients with airline tickets. You can find the tickets online yourself and have your client pay for them with a credit card. However, a host agency can provide you with the benefit of its established supplier relationships, preferred commissions, and special marketing incentives that would not ordinarily be available to you as an individual.

Setting Up

Getting started in the senior travel services business does not require a substantial amount of overhead. You can be in business with just a computer, a desk, and a phone. Chapter 13 will provide more information on how to best equip your office.

You can run your senior travel service from home or a commercial location. In fact, many storefront travel agencies have relocated to become homebased operations. Another option is to work with a local travel agency and rent desk space in its office, using its equipment and staff. Chapter 11 discusses locating and setting up in more detail.

Although this sounds like a cliché, how much money you make will depend on you. Naturally, the harder you work, the more profitable you will be. Some people see working in the travel industry as an opportunity to visit new places and take advantage of travel discounts and make a little money while they do it, while others take home $100,000-plus annually.

For more information on the nuts and bolts of starting a travel and tour business, including finding host agencies and specialty travel carriers, see Entrepreneur's *Start Your Own Specialty Travel and Tour Business*.

Policies and Procedures

Establish a comprehensive set of policies and procedures to protect you, your clients, transportation and lodging providers, and the various other entities involved in delivering travel services. The specific issues you need to address will vary depending on the type of travel service you offer.

Before your clients make a reservation, be sure they understand your cancellation policies and know what is required to receive a full or partial refund, as well as when no refund will be made. In your contract, include a "hold harmless" disclaimer that states that you are not liable or responsible for any loss, damage, injury, accident, delay, or cancellation caused by acts of God or the actions of third parties.

Reserve the right to refuse or cancel your services to anyone you feel may impede the welfare or enjoyment of other members in the tour. If there is a concern about someone's health or mental or physical condition, you can also reserve the right to refuse or cancel your services—just be sure you do it fairly and without discriminating. Have your contracts and policies reviewed by an attorney familiar with civil rights laws to make sure everything is in compliance and does not violate any local, state, or federal regulations.

To-Do List

Statistics from the Travel Industry Association of America show that the top ten activities among travelers age 55 and older are:

1. Shopping—30 percent
2. Historical places/museums—15 percent
3. Cultural events—12 percent
4. Gambling—12 percent
5. Outdoor recreation—11 percent
6. National/state parks—8 percent
7. Beaches—8 percent
8. Nightlife/dancing—5 percent
9. Theme/amusement parks—4 percent
10. Sports events—4 percent

▲

Staffing

One of the advantages to owning your own senior travel service business is that you can operate as a one-person show, performing all the tasks yourself. But if your vision is to expand and grow, you will need a plan to hire additional employees or independent contractors to assist with planning tours, booking travel packages, or handling other administrative tasks. Depending on your area of specialty, you may find that you only need extra personnel during seasonal times.

Of course, your strategy for hiring reliable staff should be addressed and included as part of your business plan. The mechanics of staffing—including finding, screening, and hiring employees; benefits; salary ranges; and other personnel issues—are discussed in Chapter 12.

Don't Quit Your Day Job

Many travel specialists start their businesses on a part-time basis that gradually evolves into a full-time operation. This allows for more flexibility, especially if you want to work around another job and keep that steady cash flow coming while you establish your online business. Also, if your current job offers a benefits package that includes insurance and retirement, that may be another incentive to keep your travel business as a part-time operation. Starting part-time gives you the opportunity to gain experience and build a solid reputation as a senior travel specialist. Some individuals continue working part-time indefinitely, while others wait until they have built up enough cash reserve to sustain them during the first year's full-time operation.

Structuring
Your Business

There's a lot to do when you start a business. This chapter will address various issues you need to deal with as you get set up.

▲

Naming Your Company

One of the most important marketing tools you will ever have is your company's name. A well-chosen name can work very hard for you; an ineffective name means you have to work much harder at marketing your company.

Your company name should very clearly identify what you do in a way that will appeal to your target market. It should be short, catchy, and memorable. It should also be easy to pronounce and spell—people who can't say your company name may use your services, but they won't tell anyone else about you.

Allen Hager chose the name of his company, Right at Home, for two reasons. First, because he runs a home care operation, he wanted a name that had a connotation of—and an emotional connection to—home. "Second, I wanted something that was very easy to remember. That is important for any kind of brand name," he says.

The Continuum was selected for Diane Ross's intergenerational health and wellness center because it refers to the "continuum of life."

Karen Martin decided to change the company name from her own name of Karen J. Martin, LLC to reflect the philosophy of this transition in time to Life Moves®. She invested in trademarking this name in two categories, costing $5,000 in filing fees and lawyer expenses. However, Martin bought the domain name lifemoves.com before filing for the Life Moves® registration mark. "Branding one's name is important for national and international recognition and reflects professionalism and credibility," she says. "Many of my clients have commented that they like the name and agree that life sure does move on!"

Though naming your company is without a doubt a creative process, it helps to take a systematic approach. Once you've decided on a name, or perhaps two or three possibilities, take the following steps:

- *Check the name for effectiveness and functionality.* Does it quickly and easily convey what you do? Is it easy to say and spell? Is it memorable in a positive way? Ask several of your friends and associates to serve as a focus group to help you evaluate the name's impact.

- *Search for potential conflicts.* Find out if any other business has a name so similar that yours might confuse the public.

- *Check for legal availability.* Exactly how you do this depends on the legal structure you choose. Typically, sole proprietorships and partnerships operating under a name other than that of the owner(s) are required by the county, city, or state to register their fictitious name. Even if it's not required, it's a good idea, because that means no one else can use that name. To find out how to register a fictitious name in your state, start by calling the local business licensing agency; they'll either be able to tell you or refer you to the correct agency. Corporations usually operate under their corporate name. In either case, you need to check with the appropriate regulatory agency to be sure the name you choose is available.

> **Bright Idea**
>
> To come up with the best name for your business, enlist the aid of family, friends, and associates by asking them to jot down names they think best describe your business. The more good minds working together, the better!

- *Check for use on the internet.* If someone else is already using your company's name as a domain name, consider coming up with something else. Even if you have no intention of developing your own website, the use could be confusing to your customers.

- *Check to see if the name conflicts with any name listed on your state's trademark register.* Your state's Department of Commerce can direct you to the correct agency. You should also check with the trademark register maintained by the U.S. Patent and Trademark Office (PTO) at uspto.gov.

Once the name you've chosen passes these tests, you need to protect it by registering it with the appropriate state agency; again, your state's Department of Commerce can help you. If you anticipate doing business nationally, you should also register the name with the PTO.

Legal Structure

One of the first decisions you need to make about your new business is your company's legal structure. This is an important decision that can affect your financial liability, the amount of taxes you pay, the degree of control you have over the company, as well as your ability to raise money, attract investors, and ultimately sell the business. However, legal structure shouldn't be confused with operating structure. The legal structure is the ownership structure (defining who actually owns the company). The operating structure defines who makes management decisions and runs the company.

A sole proprietorship is owned by the proprietor; a partnership is owned by the partners; and a corporation is owned by the shareholders. Sole proprietorships and partnerships can be operated however the owners choose. In a corporation, typically, the shareholders elect directors, who in turn elect officers, who then employ other people to run and work in the company. But it's entirely possible for a corporation to have only one shareholder and to essentially function as a sole proprietorship. In any case, how you plan to operate the company should not be a major factor in your choice of legal structures.

So what goes into choosing a legal structure? The first point is who is making the decision on the legal structure. If you're starting the company by yourself, you don't need to take anyone else's preferences into consideration. But if there are multiple people involved, you need to consider the issue of asset protection and limiting your financial liability in the event things don't go well.

Something else to think about is your prospective clients and what their perceptions will be of your structure. While it's not necessarily true, there is a tendency to believe that the legal form of a business has some relationship to the sophistication of the owners, with the sole proprietor as the least and the corporation as the most sophisticated.

Your image notwithstanding, the biggest advantage of forming a corporation is in the area of asset protection—making sure the assets you don't want to put into the business don't stand liable for the debt of the business. However, to take advantage of the protection a corporation offers, you must respect the corporation's identity. That means maintaining the corporation as a separate entity; keeping your corporate and personal funds separate, even if you are the sole shareholder; and following your state's rules regarding the holding of annual meetings and other record-keeping requirements. Do not expect a corporation to protect yourself personally against general liability issues—for example, if someone is injured on your property or suffers an injury or damages due to your negligence or some other aspect of a business transaction with you. These days, lawyers sue both the corporation and the individuals involved, so protect yourself in that area with adequate insurance.

Is any one of these business structures better than another? What's important is what's best for you. Dick Padgett and his wife simply didn't see a need to incorporate and are the sole proprietors of Five Star Concierge in San Diego.

Martin decided on a limited liability company (LLC) as a vehicle to protect her personal assets against potential litigation. "I understood that would be a way I could protect some of my personal assets," she says. "Of course, if you do something heinous, something very wrongful, then [an LLC] won't protect you. But I try very hard to be forthright and conscientious, and I chose that route."

Smart Tip

LegalZoom™ is an online legal document service provided by a team of legal experts that is a cost-effective alternative to setting up a business formation. The site walks you through each step and provides pop-up bubbles to immediately answer most of your questions. They also have customer service representatives that are available by phone. For more information go to: legalzoom.com.

Consider what you want to do now, and where you expect to take your company. Then choose the form that is most appropriate for your particular needs.

If you decide to incorporate, you may not need an attorney to set it up. There are plenty of good do-it-yourself books and kits on the market, and most of the state agencies that oversee corporations have guidelines you can use. Even so, it's always a good idea to have a lawyer at least look over your documents before you file them, just to make sure they are complete and will allow you to truly function as you want.

Finally, remember that your choice of legal structure is not an irreversible decision; although if you're going to make a switch, it's easier to go from the simpler forms to the more sophisticated ones than the other way around. The typical pattern is to start as a sole proprietor and move up to a corporation as the business grows. But if you need the asset protection of a corporation from the beginning, start out that way.

Licenses and Permits

Most cities and counties require business operators to obtain various licenses and permits to comply with local regulations. While you're still in the planning stages, check with your local planning and zoning department or city/county business license department to find out what licenses and permits you will need for your senior services operation and what is involved in obtaining them. You may need some or all of the following:

- *Occupational license or permit.* This is typically required by the city (or county, if you are not within an incorporated city) for just about every business operating within its jurisdiction. License fees are essentially a tax, and the rates vary widely based on the location and type of business. As part of the application process, the licensing bureau will check to make sure there are no zoning restrictions prohibiting you from operating in your location.

- *Health department permit.* An adult day-care center or a home care operation may need special certifications or licenses from the local health department.

- *Fire department permit.* If your business is open to the public or in a commercial location, you may be required to have a permit from the local fire department.

- *Sign permit.* Many cities and suburbs have sign ordinances that restrict the size, location, and sometimes the lighting and type of sign you can use in front of your business. Landlords may also impose their own restrictions. Most residential areas forbid signs altogether. To avoid costly mistakes, check regulations and secure the written approval of your landlord (if applicable) before you invest in a sign.

- *State licenses.* Many states require persons engaged in certain occupations to hold licenses or occupational permits. Check with your state's occupational licensing entity to find out exactly what you need based on the specific services you intend to provide.

Doug Iannelli advises entrepreneurs to be clear about their services when applying for any type of license. The first time he applied for a business license, the City of Atlanta initially declined his application because they misunderstood and thought he was trying to operate an "escort service." He went to City Hall and explained his business model was to assist, escort, and help seniors to appointments. "After showing them my marketing materials and related information, they realized I was a legitimate business and approved my business license," he says.

> **Beware!**
> Find out what type of licenses and permits are required for your business while you're still in the planning stage. You may find out that you can't legally operate the business you're envisioning, so give yourself time to make adjustments to your strategy before you've spent a lot of time and money trying to move in an impossible direction.

Business Insurance

It takes a lot to start a business—even a small one—so protect your investment with adequate insurance. If you're homebased, don't assume your homeowner's or renter's policy covers your business equipment and activities; chances are, it doesn't. If you're located in a commercial facility, be prepared for your landlord to require proof of certain levels of liability insurance when you sign the lease. And in either case, you need coverage for any inventory, equipment, fixtures, and valuables your business might own, along with liability and possibly other types of insurance.

A smart approach to insurance is to find an agent who works with businesses similar to yours. The agent should be willing to help you analyze your needs, evaluate what risks you're willing to accept and what risks you need to insure against, and work with you to keep your insurance costs down.

Typically, homebased business owners should make sure their equipment and inventory are covered against theft, fire, flood, and other perils, and that they have some liability protection if someone (either a client or an employee) is injured on their property or by their product. In most cases, one of the new insurance policies designed for homebased businesses will provide sufficient coverage. Also, if you use your vehicle for business, be sure it is appropriately covered.

In our intensely litigious society, no business owner can afford to ignore liability issues for himself or his facility. This is particularly important for operations that provide various degrees of care and supervision for elderly and possibly disabled clients. Talk to your insurance agent to evaluate your risks and determine which ones you are willing to accept and which ones you need to insure against. Most agents will help you with risk management and loss prevention; if yours is unwilling or unable to do this, find a new agent.

> **Tip...**
>
> ### Smart Tip
> When you purchase insurance on your equipment and inventory, ask what documentation the insurance company requires before you ever have to file a claim. That way, you'll be sure to maintain appropriate records, and the claims process will be easier if it is ever necessary.

Once your business is up and running, consider purchasing business interruption insurance to replace lost revenue and cover related costs if you are ever unable to operate due to covered circumstances.

In addition to property, casualty, and general liability, you may want to consider purchasing extra coverage that will pay if a claim against your basic policies exceeds their limits. This is known as an umbrella policy—it covers your other insurance.

Other potential insurance needs for your business may include accident insurance on senior clients in the event of an injury or death; vehicle insurance on any vehicles owned or leased by your business, or personal vehicles used for business purposes; and workers' compensation insurance if you have employees.

Remember, insurance will take care of the financial loss associated with a covered incident, accident, or injury, but it can't erase the pain and inconvenience. Though you need to have insurance, your goal should be to never have to file a claim.

Professional Advisors

As a business owner, you may be the boss, but you can't be expected to know everything. You'll occasionally need to turn to professionals for information and assistance. It's a good idea to establish relationships with these professionals before you get into a crisis situation.

To shop for a professional service provider, ask friends and associates for recommendations. You might also check with your local chamber of commerce or trade association for referrals.

Find someone who understands your industry and specific business and appears eager to work with you. Check out the individual and/or company with the Better Business Bureau and the appropriate state licensing agency before committing yourself.

As a provider of services to seniors, the professional service providers you're likely to need include:

- *Attorney.* You need a lawyer who practices in the area of business law, is honest, and appreciates your patronage. In most parts of the United States, you'll find many lawyers willing to compete fiercely for the privilege of serving you. Interview several and choose one you feel comfortable with. Be sure to clarify the fee schedule ahead of time, and get your agreement in writing. Keep in mind that good commercial lawyers don't come cheap; if you want good advice, you must be willing to pay for it. Your attorney should review all contracts, leases, letters of intent, and other legal documents before you sign them. He can also help you collect bad debts and establish personnel policies and procedures. Of course, if you are unsure of the legal ramifications of any situation, call your attorney immediately.

Smart Tip

Sit down with your insurance agent every year and review your insurance needs. As your company grows, it's sure to change. Also, insurance companies are always developing new products to meet the needs of the growing small-business market, and it's possible that one of these new policies will be more appropriate for you.

- *Accountant.* Among your outside advisors, your accountant is likely to have the greatest impact on the success or failure of your business. If you are forming a corporation, your accountant should counsel you on tax issues during startup. On an ongoing basis, your accountant can help you organize the statistical data concerning your business, assist in charting future actions based on past performance, and advise you on your overall financial strategy regarding purchasing, capital investment, and other matters related to your business goals. A good accountant will also serve as a tax advisor, making sure you are in compliance with all applicable regulations and that you don't overpay any taxes.

- *Insurance agent.* A good independent insurance agent can assist you with all aspects of your business insurance, from general liability to employee benefits, and probably even handle your personal lines as well. Look for an agent who works with a wide range of insurers and understands your particular business. This agent should be willing to explain the details of various types of coverage, consult with you to determine the most appropriate coverage, help you understand the degree of risk you are taking, work with you in developing risk-reduction programs, and assist in expediting any claims. Dick Padgett's insurance agent helped him research California's licensing requirements for his senior transportation service. Most companies providing passenger transportation are required to obtain a special license that requires the purchase of livery insurance as well as commercial liability. Thanks to his agent's diligence, Padgett was able to determine that he did not need the special license or the extra insurance.

- *Banker.* You need a business bank account and a relationship with a banker. Don't just choose the bank you've always done your personal banking with; it may not be the best bank for your business. Interview several bankers before making a decision on where to place your business. Once your account is open, maintain a relationship with the banker. Periodically sit down and review your accounts and the services you use to make sure you are getting the package most appropriate for your situation. Ask for advice if you have financial questions or problems. When you need a loan or a bank reference to provide to creditors, the relationship you've established will work in your favor.

> **Beware!**
> Not all attorneys are created equal, and you may need more than one. For example, the lawyer who can best guide you in contract negotiations may not be the most effective counsel when it comes to employment issues. Ask about areas of expertise and specialization before retaining a lawyer.

- *Consultants.* The consulting industry is booming, and for good reason. Consultants can provide valuable, objective input on all aspects of your business. Consider hiring a business consultant to evaluate your business plan or a marketing consultant to assist you in that area. When you are ready to hire employees, a human resources consultant may help you avoid some costly mistakes. Consulting fees vary widely, depending on the individual's experience, location, and field of expertise. If you can't afford to hire a consultant, consider contacting the business school at the nearest college or university and hiring an MBA student to help you.

- *Computer expert.* Your computer and data are extremely valuable assets, so if you don't know much about computers, find someone to help you select a system and the appropriate software, and to be available to help you maintain, troubleshoot, and expand your system as you need it. If you're going to have a website, consider hiring a professional to help you set it up.

No matter how good you are at what you do, chances are you can't do it all—and you shouldn't—so find ways to network and get in touch with professionals who can help you make your business a success.

Allen Hager advises new business owners to get involved with their local chamber of commerce and find other small-business owners who are successful in the area. "It wouldn't necessarily have to be in your industry, but find out from them who you might turn to for professional advice," he recommends.

Under Advisement

Not even the president of the United States is expected to know everything. That's why he surrounds himself with advisors—experts in particular areas who provide knowledge and information to help him make decisions. Savvy small-business owners use a similar strategy.

Advisory boards can be structured to help with the direct operation of your company and to keep you informed on various business, legal, and financial trends that may affect you.

Assemble a team of volunteer advisors to meet with you periodically to offer advice and direction. Include caregivers, volunteers, seniors, professional advisors, and other community members. Let prospective advisors know what your goals are and that you don't expect them to take an active management role or to assume any liability for your company or for the advice they offer.

When you ask for honesty, don't be offended when you get it. Your feathers may get a little ruffled when someone points out something you are doing wrong, but the awareness will be beneficial in the long run. Also, be sure to provide feedback to the board—good or bad. Let them know when you have done something based on their advice and what the results were. Finally, be willing to serve on similar advisory boards for other companies.

Let professionals help you with the activities that are essential to the profitable functioning of your business, yet are not the core of your operation. That will free you up to focus on building and growing your company.

Locating and
Setting Up

What's the ideal location for your senior
services business? It all depends on the service you provide, how
much cash you have to start, and what your goals are.
Essentially, your two choices are homebased or a commercial
location. If you opt for the latter, you'll have some additional
choices to make.

Many senior service providers start as a homebased operation and have no intention of ever moving. Others start at home with a goal to move into a commercial space as soon as they have sufficient revenue. Still others start in a commercial location.

To decide where to locate, think about what you must have to operate your business, what you'd like to have, what you absolutely won't tolerate—and how much you're able to pay. Give this process the time it needs and deserves. A poor choice of location can be an expensive mistake that's not always possible to repair.

Staying Home

One of the key benefits of a homebased business is that it significantly reduces the amount of startup and initial operating capital you'll need. But there's more to consider than simply the upfront cash. You need to be conveniently located so your clients can find you if necessary, and so you can get to them—or to other places you need to go—without spending an excessive amount of time traveling.

If your location works, consider your home from a capacity perspective. Do you have a separate room for your business, or will you have to work at the dining room table? Can you set up a comfortable workstation with all the tools and equipment you'll need? Can you separate your work area from the rest of the house so you can have privacy when you're working and get away from the office when you're not? Do you have adequate storage for inventory and supplies?

A senior relocation operation is an ideal homebased business. You will need an office area, as well as storage space for packing supplies and estate sale display items. However, a great deal of your time will be spent out of the office at your clients' homes. Karen Martin, who runs a senior moving management company in Hartford, Connecticut, says, "I'm really based at my client's house for the most part in

> **Tip...**
>
> **Smart Tip**
> Even though you're homebased, take care that you present yourself as a serious business. If clients visit your home, your office should reflect your professionalism. Also, any other areas of your home that clients may see should be neat and orderly, and create a positive impression.

terms of my work hours, or I'm at home on the computer or phone. I really do enjoy being homebased. It's nice to have that flexibility, plus it's cost effective."

Concierge, handyman, transportation, travel, and even day-care businesses can be run from either home or a commercial location, depending on the scope of your services and the size of the operation.

A homebased business offers substantial tax breaks, but you must be sure your setup meets IRS requirements. To take the home office deduction, you must have a room that is used solely as your office and/or workroom. It cannot be the corner of your family room, nor can the office do double-duty as a den or guest room.

What can you deduct? Directly related expenses, which are those that benefit only the business part of your home, and a portion of indirect expenses, which are the costs involved in keeping up and running your entire home, are eligible. For example, your office furniture and equipment are fully deductible as directly related expenses. In the area of indirect expenses, you may deduct a portion of your household utilities and services (electric, gas, water, sewage, trash collection, etc.) based on the percentage of space you use for business purposes. Other examples of indirect expenses include real estate taxes, deductible mortgage interest, casualty losses, rent, insurance, repairs, security systems, and depreciation.

> ### Smart Tip
> ## Tip...
>
> Even if your homebased office does not qualify for the home office deduction, you can still deduct other expenses—inventory, storage, equipment, shipping, automobile, marketing, etc.—that are legitimate costs of doing business.

Before you invest too much time in planning a homebased operation, check your local zoning codes and any deed restrictions that may be attached to the property. Many municipalities have ordinances that limit the nature and volume of commercial activities that can occur in residential areas. Find out what, if any, ordinances are in place regarding homebased businesses before applying for your business license.

Choosing a Commercial Location

If you decide on a commercial location, your choice should be guided largely by the services you want to provide and the market you want to reach. Starting in a commercial location requires more cash than starting from home, but the business you attract can offset the expense.

Before investing in a commercial facility, be sure the surrounding market can support the business you envision. Buying or renting a facility that can be converted to accommodate your needs will usually be much more economical than building from the ground up.

Some adult day-care centers are choosing retail space in neighborhood shopping centers. These locations typically provide easy access and plenty of parking for your clients. You might also look for space within or adjacent to an assisted-living community or near a health-care center, or investigate sharing a facility with other senior community organizations or within a retirement community. Another option is to consider space in an office or light industrial park with a sizable workforce; these workers may have parents who will become your clients.

If you are providing home care or home health care, even though your work is done at the clients' homes, you'll still need an office where you can meet with prospective clients and/or their families and have sufficient room for your administrative employees. If you are starting a transportation service, be sure you will have adequate parking to accommodate multiple commercial vehicles.

When considering commercial space, be sure the location is consistent with your style and image. Will your clients be comfortable there—whether they come regularly for day care or only occasionally to meet with you regarding other services? Is the facility accessible to people with disabilities? If you're on a busy street, how easy is it for cars to get in and out of the parking lot? Is the location easily accessible by public transportation?

If you're in a multi-tenant building, find out about the days and hours of service and access. Are the heating and cooling systems left on or turned off at night and on weekends? If you don't have your own entrance, are there periods when the exterior doors are locked, and if so, can you have keys?

> ### Bright Idea
> When looking for commercial space for a senior day-care center, check with local assisted-living facilities to see if they have unused areas in their building that you could lease. You could offer the facility's residents a discounted rate, and they might be able to prepare and deliver meals to your senior clients.

Finally, check to see if any competitors are located nearby. For a service where you go to the client—such as concierge and handyman services—it probably won't matter. But if you're going to be operating a senior day-care center, you don't want to be a block away from a similar operation. If a nearby competitor is only going to make your marketing job tougher, look elsewhere.

Walkways, Stairs, and Railings

If you are operating a senior day-care center, your facility should have safe, clearly marked pickup and drop-off points and established procedures for their use. All walking surfaces should have a nonslip finish and be free of holes and any irregularities.

All inside and outside stairs, ramps, porches, and walkways should be safe, well-lighted and constructed according to local building codes. Install handrails on both sides of stairways; the handrails should be securely attached to either the walls or the stairs.

Signage

If you're homebased, you may not be allowed to have a sign for your business—check with your local zoning board to be sure before you have one made. If you're in a commercial location, you'll definitely want to have clear, easy-to-see signs so your clients can find you.

Keep in mind that a one-inch letter is easily seen ten feet away, two-inch letters can be seen at 20 feet, and so on. Don't create a sign with letters so small that your clients can't easily read them. And keep the font simple; fancy lettering with flourishes may be hard for senior eyes to decipher.

Finally, have a professional proofreader check your sign for errors. Don't spend a lot of money just to make a poor impression.

Office Layout and Décor

A number of factors will influence how you arrange your office, including the specific business you're starting and whether you are homebased or in a commercial location. There is no one ideal layout, but the following are some points to consider.

If you are in a commercial location, you should have a small reception area. For senior day-care centers, this is where your clients can check in and out, and where their family members can wait for them if necessary. For other senior services, you need an attractive entry area to make a good first impression on your clients.

Your office décor should be businesslike, efficient, and attractive. You don't need to spend a lot of money on elegant furnishings—in fact, you shouldn't—but you do need to create a favorable impression in your clients' minds. A fresh coat of paint will go a long way in brightening up your environment. Neutral shades such as beige and muted gray are good

Smart Tip

Whether you are homebased or in a commercial location, be sure your facility has adequate electrical capacity. You'll need an ample supply of "clean" current without fluctuations, which could damage your computers or other electronic and/or medical equipment. You'll also need plenty of outlets so you can safely plug everything in. Many older office buildings and homes are lacking in this area. Consult with an electrician or a representative from your local power company to make sure the facility you're considering has the capacity to support your needs.

133

How Suite It Is

Not crazy about leasing commercial space, but can't work out of your home? An office option to consider is an executive suite, where you have your own private space, and the landlord provides receptionist and secretarial services, faxing, photocopying, conference rooms, and other support services as part of the package. Executive suites can help you project the image of a professional operation at a more affordable cost than a traditional office, and they can be found in most commercial office areas. Shop around and be sure to talk with existing tenants to be sure they're happy before signing a lease.

choices and will allow you to highlight your facility with posters, art prints, or bulletin boards.

A few large plants will also add to the ambience, but be sure you maintain them. A healthy plant is attractive and also helps to maintain clean indoor air; a wilted, droopy plant with brown leaves may make your clients wonder just how well you'll care for their family member or provide whatever other service you're offering if you can't even manage to take care of a plant.

Desks and chairs should be attractive and functional but not luxurious. Invest in ergonomically sound chairs and equipment to preserve your health and productivity, and that of your employees. Be sure trash cans are emptied regularly and that the facility is kept clean and dusted. Periodically take a look at your facility through the eyes of a client who has never seen it before and think about the impression it makes.

12

Assembling
Your Team

Most entrepreneurs will say that finding and keeping qualified employees is one of their biggest challenges. As our population ages, the labor pool is shrinking—but the demand for workers is not. This chapter will discuss some of the staffing issues that are specific to senior services operations.

When to Hire

It's a good idea to hire people before you desperately need them. Waiting until the last minute may result in hiring mistakes, which can cost you dearly, both in terms of cash and quality of care.

One key to getting and keeping good people is flexibility, and you'll find plenty of talented folks who either don't want to work full time or need to work unusual hours. If you can accommodate them, you'll both benefit. And as the workload grows and you need a full-time person doing that particular job or need to extend the hours, either change the status of that employee, or if that won't work, be creative: Consider hiring a second part-timer, setting up a job-sharing situation, or come up with some other solution that lets you to retain a valuable person and still get the work done.

Hiring Steps

The first step in formulating a comprehensive human resources program is to decide exactly what you want someone to do. The job description doesn't have to be as formal as one you might expect from a large corporation, but it needs to clearly outline the person's duties and responsibilities, such as supervising senior adults in an adult day-care setting, assisting an elderly client with meal preparation and light housekeeping, or helping a senior client downsize and sell his home. It should also list any special skills or other required credentials, such as a Certified Nurse Specialist for nurses' aides or a valid driver's license and clean driving record for someone who is going to be driving a vehicle to take senior clients to medical appointments or on errands.

Next, establish pay scales. Rates vary by geographic location and the jobs skills required. For example, the average annual wage for a home health-care aide in New York is $21,250; in Louisiana it's $19,250; and in Wyoming it's $25,100. For a registered nurse, the pay scale will be significantly higher: In South Dakota, the average annual salary for an RN is $52,800; in Florida it's $61,780; and in California it's $94,120.

You can get a good idea of the pay ranges in your area by simply checking the classified ads in your local paper. You can also compare salary ranges in your area with those in other parts of the country by going to salary.com. To find out national average pay scales for a

Beware!
Before you hire your first employee, make sure you are prepared. Have all your paperwork ready, know what you need to do in the way of tax reporting, and understand all the liabilities and responsibilities that come with having employees.

Hire Power

Before you set up the first interview with an applicant, do the following to make the hiring process as smooth as possible:

○ *Decide in advance what you need.* You know you need help, but exactly what kind of help? Do you need a caregiver or administrative support? In the very beginning, you'll be looking for people to do the tasks you can't or don't want to do. As you grow, you'll be looking for people who can help you expand your capabilities.

○ *Write job descriptions.* Take the time to put a list of responsibilities and required skills in writing. This forces you to think through what type of person will best meet your needs, which reduces the risk of hiring the wrong person. It also gives you something to show an applicant so they are able to tell if the job you are offering is the one they want.

○ *Set basic personnel policies.* Don't think that because you're a small company you can just deal with personnel issues as they come up. For example, clearly define what benefits you offer, who is eligible to receive them, and when; spell out what is unacceptable on-the-job conduct and how the disciplinary process works; explain how employees will be evaluated and what recourse workers have if they disagree with their supervisors. You'll avoid a lot of problems down the road if you set policies in advance.

variety of positions, go to the website for the U.S. Department of Labor, Bureau of Labor Statistics at bls.gov.

By offering competitive wages and benefits to employees who enjoy taking care of their senior charges, you can develop a satisfied team of employees and keep your turnover low. Diane Ross pays her staff members at her Reno, Nevada, senior adult day-care center $10 to $18 per hour, plus medical benefits and paid leave. "It's very necessary to take care of the employees [who] take care of your seniors. Then everyone is happy," she says.

You'll also need a job application form. You can get a basic form at most office supply stores or you can create your own. In any case, have your attorney review the form you'll be using for compliance with the most current employment laws.

Every prospective employee should fill out an application—even if it's someone you know, and even if they have submitted a detailed resume. A resume is not a signed, sworn statement acknowledging that you can fire them if they lie; an application is.

▲

Sample Help Wanted Notice

Director, Adult Day-Care Center

Full-Time Employment
Hours: 8 A.M. to 6 P.M.

Duties: Responsible for the overall daily operations of the Home Away From Home Adult Day-Care Center. Includes supervising staff members; updating administrative paperwork; overseeing and maintaining a safe, nurturing and healthy environment for senior adults; working with and helping caregivers to find community resources; planning recreational activities for senior adults; and promoting community awareness.

Qualifications: Must have a BA; have supervisory and administrative experience with the elderly; be computer-literate; be certified in adult CPR.

Send resume to: Julie Barker, 1234 E. 53rd St., Somewhere, CA 00000

The application will also help you verify her resume; compare the two and make sure the information is consistent.

Now you're ready to start looking for candidates.

Where to Look

Senior services business owners agree that one of their biggest challenges is finding and keeping qualified caregivers and assistants. Help-wanted ads can be expensive and may not always produce the desired response. Be creative and look for alternatives. Network among people you know, put notices on bulletin boards in churches and community areas, check with medical placement offices—in short, go to the candidates; don't wait for them to come to you. Karen Martin in Hartford, Connecticut, has a team of workers that includes close neighbors, people who have been recommended by friends and family, and even buyers who have come to her estate sales in the past.

You can also establish an extensive recruiting system as Allen Hager did for his Omaha, Nebraska, company. In addition to buying standard classified ads in the

Stat Fact

Demographic projections from the U.S. Department of Labor, Bureau of Labor Statistics, indicate that finding good employees is going to be one of the biggest challenges all businesses face for many years to come. The growth rate of the workforce is slowing down as baby boomers retire in large numbers. This means that a serious labor shortage of qualified, skilled employees could occur within the next decade.

newspaper, Hager places advertisements for Right at Home in community publications, church bulletins, and senior center newsletters; the company also has a link to a recruitment page on its website.

Your current employees can be an excellent source of referrals for new employees. Consider developing a program to pay a bonus when a candidate referred by an employee is hired and stays on the job for a particular length of time, such as six months or a year.

Evaluating Applicants

When you begin the hiring process, don't be surprised if you're as nervous at the prospect of interviewing potential employees as they are about being interviewed. After all, they may need a job—but the future of your company is at stake.

It's a good idea to prepare your interview questions in advance. Develop open-ended questions that encourage the candidate to talk. In addition to knowing what they've done, you want to find out how they did it. You might even ask them to tell you how they would handle specific situations they're likely to face while working for you. For example, ask prospective drivers what they would do if a client fell while getting out of the vehicle, or if a client wasn't waiting for the driver to arrive as scheduled. Ask each candidate for a particular position the same set of questions, and take notes as they respond so you can make an accurate assessment and comparison later.

When the interview is over, let the candidate know what to expect. Is it going to take you several weeks to interview other candidates, check references, and make a decision? Will you want the top candidates to return for a second interview? Will you call the candidate, or should they call you? This is not only a good business practice, it's also common courtesy.

Always check former employer and personal references. Though many companies are very restrictive as to what information they'll verify, you may be surprised at what you can find out. Certainly you should at least confirm that the applicant told the truth about dates and positions held. Personal references are likely to give you some additional insight into the general character and personality of the candidate; this will help you decide if he or she will fit into your operation.

Help Wanted—No Pay

To augment your staff, make use of community volunteers, who may even be seniors themselves. Volunteers can bring a wide range of skills and experiences and provide key services at virtually no cost.

Carefully screen potential volunteers by doing a thorough background check and verifying their suitability to work with seniors. Then, according to their skills and available time, match volunteers with elderly clients.

The volunteers can specify if they would enjoy working one-on-one with an elderly person or prefer to participate in group activities. Some volunteers may also be available for administrative tasks, such as answering the phone or filling out paperwork.

Finding volunteers these days is not as easy as it was in the past, with more women in the workforce and more seniors either busy traveling or caring for other family members. To recruit new volunteers, post notices at senior community centers, civic clubs, and fraternal organizations (e.g., Rotary Club), college internship programs, or in bulletins for churches, synagogues, or other places of worship. If you are not shy about speaking in front of large groups, you can ask for a few minutes to publicly make your plea at a club meeting or worship service. Send home fliers with caregivers who may know of a relative or neighbor with a little extra time on his hands.

Other things to consider are whether you want volunteers to commit to a certain day or hours a week; should they be called only as needed, or can they come to the center whenever they have free time?

When establishing a volunteer program, you will need to have specific written procedures and policies, as well as provide sufficient training and monitoring for them. Volunteers also need to be recognized for their commitment and efforts, so don't forget to let them know on a regular basis how much they are appreciated.

Be sure to document every step of the interview and reference-checking process. Even very small companies are finding themselves targets of employment discrimination suits; if it happens to you, good records are your best defense.

Check for Eligibility

Under the Immigration Reform and Control Act of 1986, you may only hire people who may legally work in the United States, which means citizens and nationals of the United States, and aliens authorized to work in the United States. As an employer, you must verify the identity and employment eligibility of everyone you hire. You must complete and retain the employment Eligibility Verification Form (I–9) on file for at least three years, or one year after employment ends, whichever period of time is longer.

The Immigration and Nationality Act protects U.S. citizens and aliens authorized to accept employment in the United States from discrimination in hiring or discharge on the basis of national origin and citizenship status.

Background Checks

Screen very carefully; negligent employees or workers temperamentally unsuited to working with the elderly can harm senior clients, damage your reputation, and be the cause of lawsuits.

Don't try to conduct background checks yourself. This is a task best left to an expert. Expect to pay anywhere from $50 to $200 for a professional background check, depending on how much detail you need. Check your telephone directory under "Investigative Services" to find a resource for background checks, or ask other business owners for a referral.

Let applicants know you will be conducting a background check to verify all their answers. Though it is unlikely that many people will admit to a history of abuse, neglect, or other inappropriate conduct, it is possible that the attention you direct to the issue will discourage them from seeking employment working with seniors. Many will not even bother to fill out an application or take the time for an interview if they know they can't pass the background check.

> **Bright Idea**
> Call local law firms and ask if they offer free newsletters or seminars on employment law or other issues that affect your operation. Most will be happy to add you to their mailing list at no charge.

Employees or Independent Contractors?

An important part of the hiring process is deciding whether you want to hire employees of your own or use independent contractors. There are advantages and disadvantages to both approaches. What's important is that you clearly understand the differences so you can avoid unnecessary and costly mistakes at tax time.

As an employer, you have greater control over employees than you do over independent contractors. Employees must comply with company policies and with instructions and direction they receive from you or a manager. You can set their hours

▲

and other conditions of employment, along with their compensation package. Of course, you must also pay payroll taxes, workers' compensation insurance, unemployment benefits, and any other employee benefits you may decide to offer.

In her moving management business, Karen Martin uses a talented team of experienced independent contractors who bring professional organization skills and in-depth knowledge of the value of items and are aware of the emotions that can arise from clients—critical talents when sorting through a house full of furnishings. Her team can range from four to ten professionals, depending on the size of the job. She prefers this type of working arrangement because she can use her workers on an as-needed basis, and they are free to work elsewhere when she doesn't need them.

If you use independent contractors, you should have a written agreement that gives a detailed description of the services the worker is to perform, the anticipated time frame in which they are to carry out those duties, and how much they will be paid. The agreement can also be instrumental in confirming that the person is indeed an independent contractor and not a salaried employee in the event the IRS or any other agency questions the working relationship. For more information, consult your accountant or tax advisor, or see Publication 15–A, *Employer's Supplemental Tax Guide*, which is available from the IRS.

Correctly classifying workers is important, and failing to do so can result in severe penalties. The fine for an intentional misclassification can be a penalty equal to 100 percent of the amount of taxes owed. The IRS is very aggressive about payroll taxes, and audits can be triggered by disgruntled former contract employees who feel they have been misclassified and decide to file a complaint.

A Family Affair

Nepotism is highly favored among small business owners; however, just because someone is a family member or close friend doesn't mean they are always the best choice. While keeping it in the family has its merits like loyalty, continuity, and dependability, there is also the danger of someone taking advantage of the working situation. However, these types of situations can be avoided if there are firm policies and procedures in place.

Anya Clowers said there were actually six additional family members who helped start her business and support her throughout the process. "Everyone has pitched in on some level," she says. This includes administrative assistance from her sister to having her son clean her house or bring her coffee, a hug, and some tissues when times were tough. "This is why I initially named my business 'Jet Travel Seven' for all of them."

Short-Term Solutions

From time to time your staffing needs may fluctuate. This can be especially true around holidays when you may have a backlog of rush orders. Perhaps a special project requires an additional person for a brief interim. Or a regular full-time staff member becomes ill or takes a vacation, leaving a vacancy for a short period.

Before the situation becomes overwhelming, consider using an employment service as a source for temporary help. Many entrepreneurs feel they can't afford the fee, but with the agency handling the advertising, screening, and background checks, their fee doesn't seem quite so large after all.

You may also find that certain tasks can be handled by an independent contractor or consultant. Consider outsourcing work in the areas of accounting and record-keeping, special marketing projects, etc. If you have tasks you need help with but that don't fit the parameters of a regular part- or full-time position, look for nontraditional ways to get them done.

Hiring Older Employees

The traditional picture of retirement is changing dramatically. "Unretirement" is a common buzzword in corporate America and it has even earned an official spot in the *Random House Unabridged Dictionary*. Increasingly, retirees are rejecting the idea of collecting the gold watch and spending their final years rocking on the porch. They're active, they're busy, and many are continuing to work. Plus, the lifting of the Social Security earnings cap has strengthened the senior labor pool and provided businesses in all industries with an excellent source of staffing.

Burwell Baker is an example of an increasing number of retirees who have unretired. Shortly after retiring as a customer representative for IBM in 1998, he re-entered the workforce as a program manager consultant. "I enjoy contributing and sharing my past experience with others," he says. "I especially appreciate not having the pressure of competing for survival in today's marketplace." And thanks to a nice retirement package, his employer doesn't need to worry about providing additional benefits beyond a decent salary.

As employees, seniors bring a plethora of experience, knowledge, expertise, and ability to the workplace. They tend to provide a higher level of customer service than their younger counterparts and often have experience that will help you with the overall management of the operation. Also, seniors are likely to stay with you longer than the worker just beginning a career. A 65-year-old who finds a job where he likes the environment, the management, and the people he works with is likely to stay with you long term, say, for another ten years, until he can no longer do the job. Another benefit of

> **Tip...**
>
> **Smart Tip**
> From the day they are hired, tell employees what they need to do to get a raise without having to ask for it; then follow up by increasing their pay rates when they've earned it.

hiring seniors is that many have their health insurance and retirement plans in place, which saves you the cost of providing these benefits.

Accommodate whatever physical limitations senior employees have as much as possible. If you notice a physical deterioration, communicate your concerns before it becomes a serious problem, and work with the employee to make adjustments in her duties if appropriate. Finally, if it becomes necessary to terminate a senior worker because of declining physical condition, try to maintain the relationship. Depending on your type of business, you might, for example, offer them limited use of your services for free or at a discount. It doesn't cost you much, but it keeps the worker feeling like a part of the organization and provides you with continued access to their knowledge base.

Once They're on Board

The hiring process is only the beginning of the challenge of having employees. You need to provide a thorough and immediate orientation for new employees.

Although many small businesses conduct their "training" by throwing someone into the job, that's not fair to the employee, and it's certainly not good for your business. If you think you can't afford to spend time on training, think again—can you afford not to adequately train your employees? Do you really want them taking care of senior adults without knowing exactly what to do?

Whether conducted in a formal classroom setting or on the job, effective training begins with a clear goal and a plan for reaching it. Training falls into one of three major categories: orientation, which includes explaining company policies and procedures; job skills, which focuses on how to do specific tasks; and ongoing development, which enhances the basic job skills and grooms employees for future challenges and opportunities. These tips will help you maximize your training efforts:

- *Find out how people learn best.* Delivering training is not a one-size-fits-all proposition. People absorb and process information differently, and your training method needs to be compatible with their individual preferences. Some people can read a manual, others prefer a verbal explanation, and still others need to see a demonstration.

- *Be a strong role model.* Don't expect more from your employees than you are willing to do. You're a good role model when you do things the way they should be done all the time. Don't take shortcuts you don't

> **Tip...**
>
> **Smart Tip**
> Do not skimp on staff. If you are operating a senior adult day-care center, there should be one caretaker for every four to six senior clients.

want your employees to take or behave in any way you don't want them to behave. On the other hand, don't assume that simply doing things the right way is enough to teach others how to do things. Role-modeling is not a substitute for training; it reinforces training. If you only role-model but never train, employees aren't likely to get the message.

- *Look for training opportunities*. Once you get beyond basic orientation and job skills training, you need to constantly be on the lookout for opportunities to enhance the skill and performance levels of your people.
- *Make it real*. Whenever possible, use real-life situations to train—but avoid letting the senior clients or their caregivers know they've become a training experience for employees.
- *Anticipate questions*. Don't assume that employees know what to ask. In a new situation, people often don't understand enough to formulate questions. Anticipate their questions and answer them in advance.
- *Ask for feedback*. Finally, encourage employees to let you know how you're doing as a trainer. Just as you evaluate their performance, convince them that it's OK to tell you the truth, ask them what they thought of the training and your techniques, and use that information to improve your own training skills.

Employee Benefits

The wages you pay may be only part of your employees' total compensation. While many very small companies do not offer a formal benefits program, more and more business owners have recognized that benefits—particularly in the area of insurance—are extremely important when it comes to attracting and retaining quality employees. In most parts of the country, the employment rate is higher than it has been in decades, which means competition for good people is stiff.

Typical benefits packages include group insurance (your employees may pay all or a portion of their premiums), paid holidays, and vacations. Some businesses offer year-end bonuses based on the company's profitability. You can build employee loyalty by seeking

Bright Idea
Find out what your employees want in the way of benefits before you spend time and money developing a package. Do a brief survey; ask what they think of the ideas you have and what ideas they have. If they want something you can't afford to do, don't reject it immediately; figure out what you can afford, and explain the situation to employees.

additional benefits that may be somewhat unusual—and they don't have to cost much. For example, if you're in a retail location, talk to other store owners in your shopping center to see if they're interested in providing reciprocal employee discounts. You'll not only provide your own employees with a benefit, but you may get some new clients out of the arrangement.

One type of insurance may not be optional. In most states, if you have three or more employees, you are required by law to carry workers' compensation insurance. This coverage pays medical expenses and replaces a portion of the employee's wages if he is injured on the job. Even if you have only one or two employees, you may want to consider offering this coverage to protect yourself and your employees in the event of an accident. Details and requirements vary by state; contact your state's insurance office or your own insurance agent for information so you can be sure to be in compliance.

Beyond tangible benefits, look for ways to provide positive working conditions. Consider establishing family-friendly policies with flexible working hours, family medical leave, and child care and/or employee assistance programs. Be sure the physical environment is pleasant, not only for the seniors but also for their caregivers, with comfortable seating, reading materials, and refreshments (e.g., coffee, tea, water).

Maintain Thorough Personnel Files

Maintaining complete and current personnel files is an important part of administering your business. Store these documents in a secure place such as a locked filing cabinet and limit who has access to them.

Personnel files are used to make job-related decisions affecting employees, and therefore should contain only information that can be legally used in making those decisions. Because federal and state law prohibits the use of sex, race, national origin, color, religion, disability, or veteran's status to make employment decisions, documents containing this information should not be included in personnel files. Similarly, medical information, garnishment orders and records, and I–9 documents should be filed separately from the employee's primary personnel file.

The personnel file on each employee should include:

- The signed and dated employment application, resume, and other hiring records
- Basic employee information: name, address, Social Security number, date of birth, job classification, work permits for minors
- A copy of your offer of employment

- All employment actions, including hires, separations, rehires, promotions, demotions, transfers, layoffs, and recalls

- A current photo of the employee which you update annually; this does not need to be a portrait—a snapshot taken with an instant or digital camera is sufficient

- Copies of any pre-employment testing, including drug test results

- Copies of all special qualifications, including licenses and certifications

- Records of any training the employee completes after coming on board

- Copies of performance reviews, commendations, and discipline or other corrective action notices

- Payroll information

- Records of any job-related illnesses and injuries

- Home address, telephone number, and emergency contact information

- For employees who drive as part of his or her job, a copy of their current, valid driver's license; for employees who use their own vehicles on the job, a copy of their current insurance certificates

> **Bright Idea**
>
> If you have employees, consider using a payroll service rather than trying to handle this task yourself. The service will calculate taxes; handle reporting and paying local, state and federal payroll taxes; make deductions for savings, insurance premiums, loan payments, etc.; and may offer other benefits to your and your employees.

The High Cost of Turnover

Employee turnover is an important issue in the senior services business industry, especially in professional caregiver and aide positions. Low wages and high stress are both factors in the industry's high turnover rate. Whatever you can do to retain good employees will help your business tremendously.

Some of the costs of turnover are fairly easy to calculate; others are essentially priceless. When someone leaves, you have the hard costs of paying overtime to other employees to get that job done until a replacement is found, of recruiting (advertising, screening, interviewing, etc.) and of training. Those numbers are fairly easy to figure. Less obvious are the decline in productivity and service quality while you are short-handed.

A key to keeping turnover down is to avoid seeing your relationship as an employer-employee one, but rather as partners. That certainly includes bonuses and profit-sharing programs, but it goes beyond pure financial incentives. Employees

Beware!
Sometimes small companies lose good employees to larger firms that have better career opportunities. They may not be attracted as much by the money and benefits as they are by the room to grow and advance. Do whatever you can to offer career growth to your staff.

need to participate in the decision-making process; they need to be encouraged to contribute ideas and solutions.

People also need to be treated with fairness and compassion. It isn't realistic to expect people to leave their personal lives at home. When employees need help dealing with family issues—whether it's as simple as taking a few hours off to watch a child perform in a play or as complex as helping an employee deal with her own elderly parent requiring full-time nursing care—it's not only kind but wise for you to provide as much assistance as possible. Along with doing the humane thing, you'll be building a level of employee loyalty that can't be bought for any amount of salary.

13

Equipping Your
Business

Many businesses providing services to seniors can be started with equipment you already own. Of course, your equipment needs for a travel service will be different than your equipment needs for a home health-care service, which is why each chapter on each type of business discusses the equipment necessary for that particular concept. In addition

▲

to specific business equipment needs, there is a wide variety of equipment for all types of operations targeting seniors that range from helpful to essential, depending on your particular situation. You don't need every single piece of equipment listed in this chapter to get started, but you should at least consider each one and decide how it works in relation to your own goals and growth strategy.

Basic Office Equipment

Many entrepreneurs find a trip to the local office supply and equipment store more exciting than a day at any mall. It's easy to get carried away when you're surrounded by an abundance of clever gadgets, all designed to make your working life easier and more fun. But if, like most new business owners, you're starting on a budget, discipline yourself to get only what you need. Consider these basic items:

- *Typewriter.* You may think that most typewriters are in museums these days, but they remain useful to businesses that deal frequently with preprinted and multipart forms and shipping documents. The determination of whether you need a typewriter is one only you can make based on your specific operation. For instance, adult day-care and home health-care services will typically have administrative, insurance, and medical forms to complete. A good electric typewriter can be purchased for $100 to $150.

- *Computer and printer.* A computer is absolutely essential for any business. It can help you manage bookkeeping and inventory control tasks, maintain client records, and produce marketing materials. Depending on your needs, you can expect to pay from $1,000 to $2,500 for a good brand-name computer or laptop, including a printer.

- *Software.* Think of software as your computer's "brains," the instructions that tell your computer how to do what you need it to do. There is a myriad of programs on the market that will handle your accounting, inventory, client information management, and other administrative requirements. Software can be a significant investment, so do a careful analysis of your own needs; then study the market and examine a variety of products before making a final decision. Many small-business owners like to use QuickBooks or Quicken software for accounting purposes, which is relatively inexpensive (approximately $60 to $250).

- *High-speed internet service.* This basically goes along with the computer because it is essential to have access to the internet. Invest in the fastest high speed internet service that your budget will allow if you anticipate transmitting a high volume of information on a regular basis. The cost for internet service widely varies with monthly costs starting at $20.

- *Surge protector.* In the event of a power failure or brownout, you'll need an uninterruptible power supply to keep your computer from going down, and a surge protector to protect your system from power surges. Even a flicker of power loss can shut down your computer causing it to "forget" all of the work you've painstakingly created during your current work session. Surge protectors generally run from $15 to $50.

- *Data protection.* You'll also need a data backup system that allows you to copy the information from your computer to another location for safe storage. A flash drive—a small memory stick device with storage capacities of 2GB to 32GB—is one of several efficient ways to make these backup chores zip right along. However, business owners have a large amount of data to back up, so an external hard drive would be the most convenient method because of how quickly they can copy the data and the amount of storage they can hold: 80GB to 2TB (1 terabyte is equal to 1,024GB).

- *Photocopier.* The photocopier is a fixture of the modern office and can be useful to even the smallest business. At the least, it will come in handy when you're making copies for your clients. The larger your operation, the more likely you are to need to make photocopies of a variety of things. You can get a basic, low-end, no-frills personal copier for less than $200 in just about any office supply store. More elaborate models increase proportionately in price. If you anticipate a heavy copy volume, consider leasing.

- *Fax machine.* As with a photocopier, the larger your operation, the greater the chance that you'll need fax capabilities. You can either add a fax card to your computer or buy a stand-alone machine. If you use your computer, it must be on to send or receive faxes, and the transmission may interrupt other work. For many businesses, a stand-alone machine on a dedicated telephone line is a wise investment. Expect to pay $90 to $250 for a fax machine.

- *Postage scale.* Most senior services operations are not heavy mail users, but if you think you might be, a postage scale is a valuable investment. An accurate scale takes the guesswork out of postage and will quickly pay for itself. It's a good idea

> **Beware!**
> Though integrated, multifunction devices—such as a copier/printer/fax machine or a fax/telephone/answering machine—may cost less to acquire and take up less space in your office, you risk losing all these functions simultaneously if the equipment fails. Also, consider your anticipated volume of use with the machine's efficiency rating and cost to operate and compare that with stand-alone machines before making a final decision.

to weigh every piece of mail—both envelopes and packages—to eliminate the risk of items being returned for insufficient postage or overpaying. Mechanical scales typically range from $15 to $30; digital scales are somewhat more expensive, generally from $45 to $200; and programmable electronic scales range from $80 to $250.

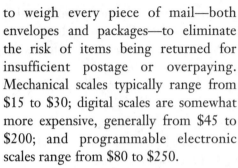

- *Postage meter.* Postage meters allow you to pay for postage in advance and print the exact amount on the mailing piece when it is used. Meters also provide a "big company" professional image, are more convenient than stamps, and can save you money in a number of ways. Postage meters are leased, not sold, with rates starting at about $20 per month. They require a license, which is available from your local post office. Only four manufacturers are licensed by the U.S. Postal Service to manufacture and lease postage meters; your local post office can provide you with contact information. You may find that buying postage online is an affordable and convenient alternative to a postage meter.

- *Paper shredder.* A response to both a growing concern for privacy and the need to recycle and conserve space in landfills, shredders are increasingly common in both homes and offices. Also, many businesses such as adult day-care facilities and home health-care services need to be compliant with Health Insurance Portability and Accountability Act (HIPAA) guidelines by disposing of protected health information with the use of shredders. They allow you to efficiently destroy incoming unsolicited direct mail, as well as sensitive internal documents, such as old client files and financial papers, before they are discarded. Light-duty shredders start at about $25, and heavier-capacity shredders run from $75 to $190.

Telecommunications

Advancing technology gives you a wide range of telecommunications options. Most telephone companies have created departments dedicated to small and home-based businesses; contact your local telephone service provider and ask to speak with someone who can review your needs and help you put together a service and equipment package that will work for you. Specific elements to keep in mind include:

- *Telephone.* Whether you are homebased or in a commercial location, two telephone lines should be adequate during the startup period. As you grow and your call volume increases, you'll add more lines.

Your telephone can be a tremendous productivity tool, and most of the models on the market today are rich in features you will find useful. Such features include automatic redial, which redials the last number called at regular intervals until the call is completed; programmable memory for storing frequently called numbers; and a speakerphone for hands-free use. You may also want call forwarding, which allows you to forward calls to another number when you're not at your desk, and call waiting, which signals you that another call is coming in while you are on the phone. These services are typically available through your telephone company for a monthly fee.

If you're going to be spending a great deal of time on the phone, consider a headset for comfort and efficiency. A cordless phone lets you move around freely while talking, but these units vary widely in price and quality, so research them thoroughly before making a purchase. You'll pay $45 to $150 for a two-line speaker phone with a variety of standard features necessary for a business.

- *Answering machine/voice mail.* Because your business phone should never go unanswered, even after regular business hours, you need a reliable answering device to take calls when you can't do it yourself. Whether you buy an answering machine (expect to pay $50 to $150 for one that is suitable for a business), or use the voice-mail service provided through your telephone company (anywhere from $15 to $20 per month) is a choice you must make depending on your personal preferences, work style, and needs.

- *Cell phone.* Once considered a luxury, cell phones have become standard equipment not only for businesspeople, but for just about everyone. Most have features similar to your office phone, and equipment and services packages are reasonably priced. Features such as digital images, text messaging, email, news services, and more are becoming increasingly available and affordable. Cell phones are especially convenient for concierge service operators, relocation specialists, transportation drivers, and others who spend a lot of time out of the office. Home care employees should also use cell phones in lieu of the client's phone for any calls not directly related to the client.

> **Dollar Stretcher**
>
> Just about any type of secondhand business equipment can be purchased for a fraction of its original retail cost. Shop the online auctions, check the classified ad section of your local newspaper, and ask new equipment dealers if they have trade-ins or repossessions for sale. Careful shopping for pre-owned items can save hundreds of dollars.

- *Toll-free number.* If you expect to have clients outside your local calling area, you may want to consider providing them with a toll-free number so they can reach you without having to make a long-distance call. Most long-distance service providers offer toll-free numbers and have a wide range of service and price packages. Shop around to find the best deal for you.

- *Email.* Email allows for fast, efficient, 24-hour communication and is an essential tool for any business. Check your messages regularly and reply to them promptly.

Other Equipment

In addition to these basics, there are other items you may need, depending on your particular operation. They include:

- *Camera.* Depending on your operation, you may find it necessary to document incidents with photographs. If an elderly person has an accident in a home health-care situation or adult day-care center, a snapshot of the scratch or injury may quickly clear up any misunderstandings. A personal concierge may want to take pictures of specific items to show the client before a final purchase is made. Travel excursions featuring groups of seniors having a blast can be photographed and shown to potential customers. You can use either a traditional film camera or a digital camera. The digital camera will provide faster results and let you see immediately if you've captured the detail you need. You have a wide range of choices regarding cameras, and new technologies are being introduced regularly.

- *Cash register.* If you have a retail operation or hold estate sales, you need a way to track sales, collect money, and make change. You can do this with something as simple as a divided cash drawer and a printing calculator, or you can purchase a sophisticated, state-of-the-art, point-of-sale system that is networked with your computer. Of course, the latter will cost somewhere between $1,200 and $5,000 per terminal and may not be a practical investment for a small startup operation. Another option is an electronic cash register, which ranges from $500 to $3,500

Dollar Stretcher

Before making a final purchase decision, shop online (both at internet stores and online auction sites such as eBay), as well as at warehouse stores, chain stores, and other suppliers to be sure you're getting the best price, quality, and service package.

and can be purchased outright, leased, or acquired under a lease-purchase agreement.

- *Credit and debit card processing equipment.* If your senior services business doesn't make retail sales, you may still want to allow your clients to pay via credit card, so you'll need a merchant account and the necessary equipment. In the adult day-care and home health-care businesses, you may have clients who appreciate the convenience of putting a credit card on file that you can charge on a monthly basis. And the majority of travel customers will prefer to pay by credit

Sign on the Dotted Line

Contracts are excellent for making sure both supplier and customer are clear on the details of the sale. This is not "just a formality" that can be brushed aside. Read all agreements and support documents carefully, and consider having them reviewed by an attorney. Make sure everything that's important to you is in writing. Remember, if it's not part of the contract, it's not part of the deal—no matter what the salesperson says. And if it's in the contract, it's probably enforceable, even if the salesperson says that never happens.

Any contract the vendor writes is naturally going to favor the vendor, but you don't have to agree to all the standard boilerplate terms. In addition, you can demand the inclusion of details that are appropriate to your situation. Consider these points when you're negotiating contracts:

- ○ *Make standard provisions apply to both parties.* If, for example, the contract exempts the vendor from specific liabilities, request that the language be revised to exempt you, too.
- ○ *Use precise language.* It's difficult to enforce vague language, so be specific. A clause that states the vendor is not responsible for failures due to "causes beyond the vendor's control" leaves a lot of room for interpretation; more precise language forces a greater level of accountability.
- ○ *Include a "vendor default" provision.* The vendor's contract probably describes the circumstances under which you would be considered to be in default; include the same protection for yourself.
- ○ *Be wary of vendor representatives who have to get any contract changes approved by "corporate" or some other higher authority.* This is a negotiating technique that generally works against the customer. Insist that the vendor make personnel available who have the authority to negotiate.

card. The equipment you need could range from a simple imprint machine to an online terminal. Credit and debit card service providers are widely available, so shop around to understand the service options, fees, and equipment costs. Expect to pay about $500 for a "swipe" machine that reads the magnetic strip on cards. You'll also pay a transaction charge, which might be a flat rate (perhaps 20 to 30 cents per transaction) or a percentage (typically 1.6 to 3.5 percent of the sale).

Dollar Stretcher

Ask suppliers if payment terms can be a part of your price negotiation. For example, can you get a discount for paying cash in advance?

On page 157, you'll find an Equipment and Supplies Shopping List. Use this as a guideline when you go shopping for your business' supplies and equipment.

Security

Whether you are homebased or in a commercial location, you need to be sure that your facility is safe and secure for you, your employees, and your clients. And, of course, you also want to protect your equipment and any inventory you might have.

Begin by investigating your area's crime history to determine what kind of security measures you need to take. To learn whether your proposed or existing location has a high crime rate, check with the local police department's community relations department or crime prevention officer. Most will gladly provide free information on safeguarding your business and will often personally visit your site to discuss specific crime prevention strategies. Many also offer training seminars for small businesses and their employees on workplace safety and crime prevention.

The cost of electronic surveillance equipment is dropping thanks to technology, and installing such security devices may earn you discounts on your insurance. You can also increase the effectiveness of your security system by discreetly posting signs in your windows and around your facility announcing the presence of the equipment.

Purchasing

No matter how smart a consumer you are, when it comes to business purchasing, you're playing a whole new game. The rules are different and the stakes significantly higher. But correctly done, purchasing—or procurement—will increase your net income.

Equipment and Supplies Shopping List

Use the following checklist as a shopping guide to get your office set up. Each item listed is not necessarily required before you start, but even if you don't buy it now, you might want to have it eventually.

❑ Computer system (with printer, plus extra printer cartridge)
❑ Digital camera
❑ Fax machine and extra ink cartridge
❑ Typewriter
❑ Postage scale
❑ Paper shredder
❑ Two-line full-featured phone system with answering machine
❑ Cell phone
❑ Camera
❑ Cash register
❑ Uninterruptible power supply
❑ Flash drive or external hard drive
❑ Surge protector
❑ Calculator
❑ Photocopier
❑ Desk
❑ Desk chair
❑ Printer stand
❑ File cabinet(s)
❑ Bookcase
❑ Computer/copier paper
❑ Business cards
❑ Letterhead, regular paper, and envelopes
❑ Address stamp
❑ Mouse pad
❑ Miscellaneous office supplies
❑ Toll-free number
❑ Voice mail
❑ Email

Choosing Suppliers

Whether you're buying items for your inventory, a major piece of office equipment, or a toner cartridge for your laser printer, you should evaluate each vendor on quality, service, and price. Look at the product itself, as well as the supplementary services and support the company provides.

Verify the company's claims before making a purchase commitment. Ask for references, and do a credit check on the vendor, which will tell you how well the supplier pays his own suppliers. This is particularly important for inventory sources, because it could ultimately affect you. If your vendor is not paying his own vendors, he may have trouble getting materials, and that may delay delivery on your order. Or he may simply go out of business without any advance notice, leaving you in a lurch. Also confirm the company's general reputation and financial stability by calling the Better Business Bureau, any appropriate licensing agencies, trade associations, and Dun & Bradstreet at dnb.com.

A major component of the purchasing process is the supplier's representative, or salesperson. The knowledge and sophistication level of individual salespeople often depends on the product or industry; however, they can be a tremendous source of education and information. Some businesspeople dismiss sales reps with an attitude of "I don't have time to see peddlers," but this is a mistake. Make it a rule to treat all salespeople with courtesy and respect, but insist that they do the same for you. You can, for example, set and enforce a policy that salespeople are seen only by appointment, or at certain hours. You can also ask them in advance how much time you need to allot for your meeting, and stick to that schedule.

Besides telling you what they have, salespeople should be asking questions. A good salesperson will try to find out what your needs are and how his company can satisfy them. As in the consumer sales arena, commercial salespeople use both high- and low-pressure tactics. Consider studying sales techniques so you can recognize and respond to the methods being used with you.

Bright Idea

If your storage space is limited, try negotiating a deal like this with your suppliers: Make a long-term purchase commitment to earn volume pricing, but arrange for delivery in increments so you don't have to store the materials.

Bright Idea

If you have employees, get their input when making purchasing decisions on supplies and equipment. The people who are using these items every day know best what works and what doesn't, what's efficient and what isn't.

Building Strong Supplier Relationships

Reliable suppliers are an asset to your business. They can bail you out when you make an ordering mistake or when your clients make difficult demands on you. But they will do so only as long as your business is profitable to them. Suppliers, like you, are in business to make money. If you argue over every invoice, ask them to shave prices on everything they sell you, or fail to pay your bills promptly, don't be surprised when their salespeople stop calling on you or refuse to help you when you're in a bind.

Of course, you want the best deal you can get on a consistent basis from your suppliers. Just keep in mind that no worthwhile business arrangement can continue for long unless something of value is rendered and received by all involved. The best approach is to treat your suppliers the way you would like your customers to treat you.

Find out in advance what your suppliers' credit policies are and pay within their terms. Most will accept credit cards but will not put you on an open account until they've had a chance to run a credit check on you. They may ask you to provide a financial statement; if they do, don't even think of inflating your numbers to cover a lack of references. This is a felony, and it's easily detected by most credit managers.

If you do open an account with a supplier, be sure you understand the terms and preserve your credit standing by paying on time. Typically, you'll have 30 days to pay, but many companies offer a discount if you pay early.

Building Your
Online Presence

Today, an internet presence is as essential as a phone and fax machine. A website is your online brochure and it will be working for you 24 hours a day, seven days a week. In addition to credibility, a professional looking website gives you a variety of marketing opportunities.

Developing a website is crucial to gaining new business. Many baby-boomers find Karen Martin on the internet with a few key search words when they are faced with orchestrating their parent's move. Martin used a talented, experienced senior in high school to create her first website. The cost was a total of $1,500 and her time in writing the content.

Whether you decide to set up and design your own website or hire someone to do it for you, there are some things you need to think about in advance.

Registering Your Domain Name

The first and most important step for online presence is registering a primary domain name. This is the first thing that pops up when someone is doing an online search for your business. The domain name of your website should be practical and, if possible, carry the same name as your business. At the very least, it should reflect the nature of your services. It should also be 22 characters or less so it's easy for people to remember. The fewer the characters, the less likely it is that someone will make a mistake typing the address into his browser.

> **Tip...**
>
> **Smart Tip**
> Visit Nameboy.com (nameboy.com) to find clever and interesting domain names in your area of specialty. This is a great free nickname generator that can be used for finding names for almost anything, although it is primarily used to find domain names for websites. Simply type in two keywords that best describe your business and let Nameboy do the rest.

The next step is to register your domain name as quickly as possible before someone else beats you to the punch. This can be done through many different venues including GoDaddy.com, Register.com, and NetFirms .com. Different registrars charge different prices and offer a variety of packages, so look closely at several to see which one best suit your needs.

Beware!
If someone else registers your domain name such as your ISP or another agency, make sure they don't inadvertently register the domain in their name and not yours. This common practice can cause a lot of problems down the road, especially if they let it lapse or sell it to someone else.

New domain registrations typically cost $12 to $99 per year, which generally includes free parking (in the absence of a website), several email accounts, mailing lists, and other ecommerce options. Some of the packages may also include website hosting for free or a nominal fee.

The person registering the domain, the technical contact, and administrator can all be the same person; just remember to provide up-to-date contact information. You should also take this opportunity to make the registration information private by "locking" it—usually for an additional fee. Not only will this prevent spammers from looking up your personal information in the WHOIS database, but it will thwart someone else from stealing and transferring it.

Planning Your Site

Before getting bogged down with elaborate web design details, business writer Melissa Campanelli advises entrepreneurs to first sit down and construct a well-thought-out website plan. "An outline helps you get the most out of your e-commerce budget," she writes. "You'll know whether you or someone in your company can each do a piece or if you need outside help." Plus, if you decide to outsource some (or all) of the project, a detailed outline will be beneficial to a professional web designer.

In her book, *Open an Online Business in 10 Days* (Entrepreneur Press), Campanelli provides the following tips for preparing an effective website outline:

Content

The key to a successful site is content. Give site visitors a lot of interesting information, incentives to visit and buy, and ways to contact you. Once your site is up and running, continually update and add fresh content to keep people coming back for more.

Structure

Next, structure your site. Decide how many pages to have and how they'll be linked to each other. Choose graphics and icons that enhance the content. Pictures of retirees on a cruise ship playing shuffleboard, for example, might work well if you're promoting travel packages. Visitors can click to jump to other pages within the site where they can find more information or book a cruise online.

At this point, organize the content into a script. Your script is the numbered pages that outline the site's content and how pages flow from one to the next. Page 1 is your home page, the very first page that site visitors will see when they type in your website address, or URL. Arrange all the icons depicting major content areas in the order you want them. Pages 2 through whatever correspond to each icon on your homepage.

Writing a script ensures your website is chock-full of great content that is well organized. Write well, give site visitors something worthwhile for their time spent with you, and include a lot of valuable information and regular opportunities to get

▲

more content. Whether you offer a free newsletter, a calendar of events, health columns from experts or travel reviews, content and its structure become the backbone of your website.

Design

With the content and structure in place, site design comes next. Whether you're using an outside designer or doing it yourself, concentrate on simplicity, readability, and consistency. Before you start using HTML tags right and left, remember what you want to accomplish. Keep surfing the internet to research what combinations of fonts, colors, and graphics appeal to you, and incorporate pleasant and effective design elements into your site. Those little subtleties make all the difference in how visitors respond to your website.

Navigation

Make it easy and enjoyable for visitors to browse the site. Use no more than two or three links to major areas, never leave visitors at a dead end, and don't make them back up three or four links to get from one content area to another. For example, if you have a website for senior concierge services, make it easy for visitors to visit other pages within your website where they can find information about your company, specific services, rates, whom to contact, articles, current events, and more.

Credibility

This is an issue that shouldn't be lost in the bells and whistles of establishing a website. Your site should reach out to every visitor, telling her why she should buy your product or your service. It should look professional and give potential customers the same feeling of confidence that a phone call or face-to-face visit with you would. Remind the visitors that you don't exist only in cyberspace. Your company's full contact information—contact name, company name, street address, city, state, zip code, telephone number, fax number, and email address—should appear on your home page.

> **Bright Idea**
>
> Get inspiration for website design ideas by checking out *PC Magazine's* Top 100 Websites (go.pcmag.com/topwebsites). You can also find the Criteria for Website Excellence at 100Best WebSites.org/criteria.htm, which identifies 21 criteria they use when selecting top sites.

Design Essentials

In today's internet climate, putting together a professional looking site is a relatively easy task, especially with the numerous tools and services available. However, knowing how to structure it and pull everything together may not be as straightforward as you might hope.

The first rule of thumb is to keep things simple for curb appeal and ease of navigation. If you start loading up your site with flashy videos and audio features, many of your visitors are going to feel overwhelmed, especially if they are on dial-up and it takes forever for your homepage to download. Plus other computers are not always equipped with the appropriate plug-ins, so a separate download may be needed to view some of your site.

If you really feel strongly about using Flash-animated graphics and banners on your site, create two versions that visitors can opt to use from an introduction splash page. The basic version would be developed for people who have a slower, dial-up connection without all of the bells and whistles. The Flash-enabled site would be designed for folks who have high-speed internet access and can view the special features without any problems.

Another consideration is having your site compatible with the major web browsers: Internet Explorer, AOL, Safari, and Mozilla's FireFox. Web pages look different from one browser to the next, so it's important to test each page before uploading them to the internet.

Hosting Your Site

Now that you have this great website put together and ready to launch, let's talk about your hosting options. Unless you plan on hosting it yourself (not a typical option due to cost and operational factors), you will need to find a reliable web host provider.

A web host stores your website, including graphics, and transmits it to the internet for other users to view. Not all web hosts are created alike, so shop around for one that has the best package for your needs. Some will include freebies such as domain registration, design templates, or no setup fees. And most hosts provide combination packages that can include site-building tools, content management, shopping carts, product catalogs, tracking and reporting capabilities, email accounts, and more.

Depending on how much disk space you need, basic hosting service can start as low as $8 per month. How do you determine the amount of disk space your site requires? It really depends on the size and number of images you have on your site. Most sites do not use more than 10MB of storage, and most web hosts offer between 10MB and 35MB of free storage with the option to upgrade. But if you are still in doubt, check with a computer consultant before committing yourself to a specific plan.

You Get What You Pay For

Free is good, right? Not when it comes to website hosting. A "free" host is never actually free. The host has to make money somehow, and the most common way is with those annoying, flashy banners and pop-up sponsor ads that have absolutely nothing to do with your business but are going to be the first thing visitors to your site see. You have no control over the ad content, and some of it can be inappropriate. You'll also find that most free hosts offer little, if anything, in the way of technical support.

Free sites are typically limited in the amount of space you have. Most allow no more than three pages and minimal use of graphics, resulting in plain, unprofessional-looking sites without the extras that a paid host provides. Finally, your URL will be long and clearly indicative of the fact that you are operating from a free site such as: myfreewebhost.myseniorservicessite.com. Unfortunately, this does little to inspire confidence in your customers.

A good web host doesn't have to be expensive. There are a lot of good, affordable hosting services out there, and many provide packages that include a registered domain name, professionally designed templates, secure services, email boxes, online or phone support, and more.

Optimizing Your Website

Ever wonder why certain sites keep popping up at the top of a search query whenever keywords are used? Is there a secret to earning higher search engine rankings? Not really; at least not in the same sense as national security secrets or breaking the magician's code style of secrets. The real secret is learning how search engine rankings work, which is primarily providing relevant keywords, coherent new content and steadily increasing your incoming links. Fortunately, this information is widely available and we're going to try to condense some of it in this chapter by providing tips about Search Engine Optimization (SEO), as well as free and fee-based marketing strategies.

According to a report from the Pew Internet & American Life Project— which provides reports measuring the impact of the internet—71 percent of American adults use the internet. Of that percentage, at least 91 percent use search engines to find information online. Even without those statistics everyone basically knows that people conduct online searches by entering specific keywords into a search engine's search box. But what most people don't know is how some of these sites consistently turn up on the first and second pages of the search results.

Statistics indicate that people will not venture past the second or third page of search results; therefore, you have to think like your targeted visitor. Ultimately, the goal is for your site to appear in the top 20 search results (ideally top 10).

To get the maximum benefit of a website, you want it to rank as high as possible in the results when a user conducts an online search. One way to increase your site's visibility is to make it "bot-friendly." The term refers to the "robots" or "spiders" that search engines send crawling through the internet, scavenging information from websites that is indexed for searches. The more information those electronic researchers can access from your site, the higher your ranking will be.

Understanding Keywords

The use of targeted keywords is essential in promoting your site through search engine optimization. So, think about what keywords or phrases you would type in a search engine to find a website selling your senior services. The first few keywords will be rather obvious. If the purpose of your website is to promote transportation services, then words and phrases like "assisted elder transportation" and "senior transportation" will be your first words to target. However, there are hundreds of sites promoting senior services so you will need to streamline your search to include particular special needs.

Next, consider other unique, related words your audience might decide to look for, such as "downsizing a home" or "estate liquidation." These are just a sample of the many unique keywords Karen Martin uses on her Life Moves site (lifemoves.com).

Plan to use different keywords on various pages of your website. For example, like Martin, devote an entire page to tips and resources on how to prepare for moving to a new home. Use these keywords with other pages to create a complete website that focuses on all aspects of a particular topic.

Make a list of 25 keywords and phrases that apply to your site, including plural and past tense versions, as well as synonyms. From the list, select a primary and secondary keyword or phrase for one of your web pages. The primary keyword should appear in the title tag, main heading, content of the text, and the linking URL. The secondary keyword should appear in one or two subheadings and throughout the text.

When it comes to content, search engines seem to rank pages higher with relevant keywords in the opening paragraph. A good rule of thumb is to write your content like newspaper journalists who generally summarize the angle of the story at the beginning.

The best way to score a high ranking on the search engines is to provide good, relevant content on your website using unique keywords. Keep the word count around

▲

500 or less and don't stuff the page with keywords. Otherwise, the search engines will toss your page into the abyss without cataloging it—they hate spam. They also hate it when webmasters resort to other forms of trickery like using hidden keywords or links (done by making the text teeny-tiny and the same color as the background so only the spiders can see it), or insert irrelevant links or keywords. They will also ban you from future searches if you copy another website's content.

Link Building Strategies

Search engines track how many other websites point back to your site. The more sites featuring your site's URL, the higher your site will rank in search results, right? Well, not exactly. You've probably heard the old adage, "You are judged by the company you keep." This definitely applies to what sites you link to. Whether you are trading links with another site or including their hyperlinks in your site's content, you want to make sure theirs is a high quality website that is relevant to your own. If you link to mismatched or inappropriate sites just for the sake of getting backlinks, you will actually do your site a disservice.

Incoming Links (aka Backlinks)

Acquiring quality inbound links is an extremely important part of the SEO process. The more quality sites you have pointing to your site, the better. Note the emphasis on "quality." If the link is coming from a spammy type of site who is trying to acquire hundreds of links in the hopes it will raise their visibility, that doesn't help you at all. However, if the backlink is from a highly reputable site in your niche, that has more clout and gives you higher visibility.

Outgoing Links

Relevant outgoing links to other sites play a part in the ranking process with search engines. If you don't have any outgoing links, your site will be considered a dead end, and why would the search engines want to send anyone to a

Get Connected

Here are additional tips for how to acquire more links:

○ *Search engines.* Submit your site to all of the major search engines. Make sure to read their submission guidelines before proceeding so that your site doesn't get bumped out of line.

○ *Provide good content.* Give people a reason to link to you by making sure your site's content is useful. Informative and well-written content will always be linked to by other sites. Strategically use keywords and phrases so no one will guess that the text has been optimized for the search engines. Also, the more content the better—but not all on the same page. The more web pages you have indexed with different keywords, the better your chances of showing up in an online query.

○ *Alert the media.* Send out a press release featuring your site and URL. Submit to online press release services like PRWeb (prweb.com) or to an RSS online generator like the one found at RSS Specifications (rss-specifications .com/rss-submission.htm).

○ *Link exchange directories.* Participating with a link exchange program works pretty much like reciprocal links. Just make sure to use niche directories that specifically relate to your business. This should be a carefully done process that is hands-on. In other words, don't use an automatic submission program.

○ *Give away freebies.* Offer visitors a free e-book, report, or other type of product from your website. Other sites often link back to sites offering freebies if they think their visitors or subscribers would benefit.

○ *Ask.* Look at who your competitors are linking to and see if that site would be willing to give you a backlink. The worst that will happen is they may say, [no].

○ *Internal linking.* Be careful to do a thorough job internally linking the pages in your website. If you naturally point to various pages in your site you will increase your chances of search engines following the links and finding additional pages to index. Periodically test your links. The spiders greatly dislike broken links, which is a sign of sloppy web design.

dead end? They want to send visitors to sites that will supply more information, including useful links. By linking to other sites, you are demonstrating your familiarity with a specific topic and that you know enough to recommend other sources of information. Always carefully check out a site before linking to it. Not only should that site be complementary to yours, but it should also be listed in the search engines. If you are still unsure and don't feel comfortable, don't link.

Reciprocal Links

These are text links or banner ads that are swapped with another website owner. This can be done through link exchange programs or by contacting the website owner directly and asking for an exchange. Many sites feature a "favorite links" page with partners they are exchanging links with. Reciprocal links are better than no links at all, but one-way links (incoming) are the best. Many of the search engines keep track of how many sites point back to your link. The more sites that promote your business, the higher visibility your website will have when someone does a search.

Listing Your Website

Search engines make it their number one goal to discover and index all of the content available on the internet to provide surfers with the best search experience. And the major ones such as Google and Yahoo! use the free crawl process to stay abreast of new and updated sites. Technically, you don't have to do a thing to get noticed by these search engines because the electronic spiders will eventually find you. The question is when? Since you probably don't want to wait for them to find you six months down the road, go ahead and get a head start by submitting your URL to the four major search engines:

1. *Google (google.com).* This search engine was chosen four times as the Most Outstanding Search Engine by Search Engine Watch (searchenginewatch.com) readers. It is also used to provide AOL search results.
2. *Yahoo! (yahoo.com).* Considered the internet's oldest directory, Yahoo! implements its own crawler-based search technology with specialized search options for browsers.
3. *Bing (bing.com).* Formerly Live Search. This search engine has new innovative features including a social feature "sidebar" that searches users' social networks for information relevant to the search query.
4. *Ask* (ask.com). Formerly AskJeeves.com, there is not a free way to submit your website to this search engine. Unless you are willing to participate in the PPC-based sponsored listing program, you will have to wait for its crawlers to find you.

When you submit your website to one of the major search engines, go ahead and include one or two additional pages along with your homepage. Typically, search engines index your other pages by following the links you provide. However, sometimes pages get missed. Therefore, you should submit the top three pages that best represent your entire website. These alternative web pages can also serve you in case your primary index page is not working properly. It is also recommended that you personally submit your site to search engines so you can take note of any problems reported. Entrusting this to a service, or even an automatic submission program, is not the wisest move.

> **Smart Tip**
> Be sure your web address is printed on your business cards, all your promotional materials and all your ads. You might also include it in your after-hours voice mail announcement.
>
> **Tip...**

Another often-ignored point is that webmasters should resubmit their site after making major changes to their web pages. While search engines revisit sites periodically, some are smart enough to realize that many pages only change once or twice a year. Therefore, a search engine may limit periodic visits to a semi-annual basis. By resubmitting your pages immediately after republishing them, you can help your site to stay current with major search engines—and thus improve in the rankings.

Blogging for Business

In addition to having a website, you can also benefit from having a blog which increases your online exposure to a broad range of potential clients by providing articles and tips for seniors related to your industry. By regularly posting information on your blog you will automatically improve your search rankings, plus it lets you build brand-awareness with visitors. Regular blogging also gives you the opportunity to differentiate yourself from the competition, exploit any niches, manage your own professional reputation and position yourself as an authority in your field. Connect your blog with social networks such as Facebook and Twitter, and you will increase your exposure exponentially.

You can also contact other highly recognized blog owners within your niche or specialty, and offer to write a guest post that will link back to your site.

Essentials of
E-Marketing

Many business owners do not enjoy the

prospect of marketing whether online or not, but it can actually

be a lot of fun as you devise clever and innovative ways to fill

the coffers. To help you do that, the next two chapters will pro-

vide different marketing tips, tricks, and techniques that will encourage prospective clients to take a closer look at your senior services. They will also help you identify the competition and how to rise above it.

Whether you're on a shoestring budget or have a boatload to spend on marketing, you've got lots of options. The most important thing to keep in mind about marketing is this: It's not an expense; it's an investment in your business.

The internet has become the number one place people turn to when researching different types of services and products, so you need to do everything you can to make sure your business is found.

There isn't a single marketing technique that is a one-size fits all. You need to try a variety of strategies to see which works best for your business such as search engine optimization, pay-per-click ad campaigns, writing articles, and sending out news-based press releases on a regular basis.

The American Marketing Association (marketingpower.com) defines marketing as "the process of planning and executing the conception, pricing, promotion, and distribution of ideas, goods, and services to create exchanges that satisfy individual and organizational goals." This means you have to apply different solutions to different circumstances.

Google AdWords—What They Are and How to Use Them

Google is not only one of the biggest and most widely used search engines in the world; it is also one of the most lucrative means of advertising in any medium. Like the other search engines, Google tries to keep the competition fair by showing favoritism toward websites that provide thoroughly original content, relevant keywords, and massive linking with other sites. However, guaranteeing a number one ranking on a Google search can be difficult because many factors come into play. To give website owners a different advantage, paid placements are offered as an alternative. Basically, every major search engine accepts paid listings, which are usually marked "Sponsored Links."

Google AdWords (adwords.google.com) are keyword generated text ads. They have been proven to be an effective form of online advertising because they have a much higher click-through-rate (CTR) than the flashy, colorful banner ads. Most internet users suffer from a condition called "banner blindness." They refuse to be distracted from their primary objective to seek and find; therefore banners are often ignored. Text ads on the other hand are outperforming banner ads five to one because they are specifically targeting the browser who is searching for something in particular, plus they are easy and relatively inexpensive to implement. Doug Iannelli says that

Smart Tip

Sign up for Google Alerts (google.com /alerts) to find out who is talking about you and your business online. This handy service also helps you keep tabs on a competitor or get the latest news and events on a particular topic.

Google AdWords have been helpful in promoting his two businesses, Flying Companions and Appointment Companions.

This concept harkens back to the old-fashioned way of advertising when companies outbid one another for the opportunity to show a commercial on television. This is essentially what Google AdWords represents: a pay-per-click (PPC) system of advertising technology with participants bidding on select keywords and phrases. When a potential customer types specific keywords into a Google search engine, relevant text ads (known as "contextual advertisement links") appear either on the side or above the natural search results.

The advantages of using Google AdWords are many. Your senior services website will be separated from the common results page and will reach local customers, as well as national and even worldwide audiences. The disadvantages of using this feature lie mainly in the limitations. The biggest limitation is that you can only write short blurbs about your product or service, typically one or two sentences.

What Determines the Order of Paid Listings?

Theoretically, your ad is placed in accordance with how much you are willing to pay for each click. However, Google has taken the process a step further by taking into account the number of times an ad impression that has been generated by a particular keyword or phrase is clicked, in addition to the amount an advertiser is willing to pay. So even if you paid less than Daddy Warbucks for a keyword but your ad generated more clicks, you could go to the front of the line and have your ad promoted ahead of his.

The determining factor is the overall quality score. This is calculated through historical click-through rates as well as the relevance of the website's ad according to text phrase. Therefore, while this system is largely money-based, there are still guidelines to be followed. After all, Google gets paid every time a web surfer clicks on one of the ads, so they want to ensure a strong click-through rate.

It should also be understood that impressions are free. The term "impression" means whenever a surfer sees your advertisement. No matter how many times your AdWord appears on a website or search results page, you are not charged anything until it is clicked. Of course, the objective is to encourage potential customers to click your ads as often as possible. If your advertising campaign fails to attract a moderate to high quantity of clicks, then Google will lose money and possibly deactivate your keywords.

When you use Google AdWords your intent is not merely to get impressions or even direct links to your website. Your objective is to promote your services, therefore justifying the expense of using Google AdWords. This can be done by giving browsers a strong call to action in your short, limited blurb.

Google has made internet advertising not only easy, but also very affordable to the average consumer who is new to the internet and does not have a large amount of capital to invest in marketing. Make a little money for Google, and the world's most popular search engine can make a little more money for you.

Article (or Bum) Marketing: Why It's *Still* Great for Business

Article marketing is a low-cost form of advertising in which someone writes a short article related to some aspect of their business, which is then tied into their service or product. Once the article has been written, it's freely distributed online or in print publications. Immediately following the article is the author's biography that includes contact information, references, the name of the business—and most importantly, the site's URL.

These freely distributed articles can expand your credibility within the senior industry and also reap some free publicity. This model of marketing has actually been in existence for decades—as long as there has been any sort of mass printing process. For example, when newspapers and magazines were only available in print, a business owner may have written a useful article for the newspaper free of charge. In return, the publication provided the writer's contact information. Since the internet has reconstructed how businesses operate in recent years, the need of article marketing has steadily increased. Many websites are looking for free content, and authors who have services or products to promote can certainly see the benefit in writing free material.

When the article is ready for publication, it's then submitted to popular article websites and directories—unless this task has been passed on to a SEO marketing service. Then website and blog owners, as well as ezine publishers pick it up and place it on their sites, which helps it climb up the ranks of the search engines. When a prospective customer sees the article and identifies the author (you) as an authority in that particular field, they will feel comfortable using the senior services you are subtly promoting.

Even with Google's continual algorithm updates, there are still many advantages to this type of online marketing when it's done correctly by providing material that is relevant and written for human eyes—not search engine crawlers.

> **Fun Fact**
> Article marketing is affectionately called "bum marketing" because the concept is so simple even a bum off the street could do it.

Submitting to Article Directories

When submitting your article to article directories, remember that your ultimate goal is to provide free content to webmasters and bloggers who appreciate a well-written story and will reprint your article on their blog or website. One high-quality article is usually more effective than a hundred articles full of gibberish, especially if this one article is posted on a highly ranked website. In exchange for quality traffic, article marketing need not be "bum marketing"— not if you have something important to share with the world—along with your contact information, of course.

Here are some of the more popular article directories to look at:

- ❍ Article Dashboard—articledashboard.com
- ❍ Author Connection—authorconnection.com/
- ❍ Blogger Linkup—bloggerlink.com
- ❍ Ezine Articles—ezinearticles.com/
- ❍ GoArticles—goarticles.com
- ❍ HubPages—hubpages.com
- ❍ Idea Marketers—ideamarketers.com
- ❍ iSnare—isnare.com
- ❍ myBlogGuest—myblogguest.com
- ❍ Search Warp—searchwarp.com
- ❍ Squidoo—squidoo.com
- ❍ WikiHow—wikihow.com

How Search Engine Optimization Ties In

Obviously, the higher ranked an article or page is the more traffic it will draw. This also means a greater chance of increased sales. One of the most important lessons in learning SEO and getting higher earnings is acquiring more HTML links pointing back to your site from other websites. This is why syndicated articles often link back to a business owner's website within the biography box. Having these links is one of the most important ways to improve your search rankings.

Unfortunately, there are problems with article marketing, specifically the quality of syndicated articles. Many have been poorly written and are a far cry from the syndicated articles that appear in newspapers. Why the low quality? Too often web owners create the article exclusively for SEO purposes, which means that the articles have either been reprinted or stuffed full of keywords without much thought to coherency. Then there are business owners who will write pretty much anything for the sole purpose of submitting the articles to directories in the hopes of gaining recognition.

Some experts speculate that the low quality of articles has resulted from the sudden popularity of article marketing, and thus the rushed production of articles. Others fault writers for poorly researching information or for having no particular experience with a particular subject. These articles may get rapid exposure for a business, but in the end the marketing campaign will be unsuccessful. Web viewers are not stupid and notice if the author has no idea what he is talking about. Therefore, it pays to be informed about the subject you are writing about. It may involve producing higher quality work by thoroughly researching a subject or hiring freelance writers to do the job more effectively.

The Benefits of Social Networking

It's true that "time is money," and time spent networking online is critical to the success of promoting your business online. This is a low- or no-cost marketing strategy that can have a global impact while building personal relationships and credibility. Many entrepreneurs have joined this growing trend and are promoting themselves via social networks like Facebook (www.facebook.com), LinkedIn (www.linked in.com), and Google+ (www.plus.google.com). It's not at all unusual for one entrepreneur to ask another, "Do you twitter?" while referring to the wildly popular microblogging service (www.twitter.com) that allows members to send short updates or "tweets" to other users.

Participating on other popular networking sites such as Pinterest (www .pinterest.com), YouTube (www.youtube.com), and Instagram (www.instagram.com), will provide good search results when others are looking for you, which makes them great resources for maximizing cross promotion for your business.

Other types of online communities that have been around since the 1990s are listservs (email distribution lists), discussion forms, newsgroups, bulletin boards, and chat rooms. These are still great opportunities to become known as an expert in your field and drive traffic to your website. Google, Yahoo!, and AOL all have special interest groups that millions of people regularly interact on. Also, many organizations related to the senior industry have discussion forums that members can network on.

While it's true that social networking can be time consuming, it can also be very effective when done consistently. Set aside a specific time each day to participate in relevant discussion forums and newsgroups so that you are not easily sidetracked. The biggest investment will be your time, so you don't want to waste it.

> **Smart Tip**
>
> One of the best ways to promote your business in emails and on discussion boards is by providing direct links in your signature line. This simple marketing technique works as an unobtrusive promotional pitch—almost like a virtual business card. Keep it short with no more than two to three lines that include a link to your website or affiliate landing page.

Online Newsletters

> **Beware!**
>
> With just a few keystrokes you can find hundreds of websites selling email addresses by the thousands. While the temptation to quickly build up your customer database is great, don't do it. These email addresses are usually "harvested" and in non-compliance with the CAN-SPAM Act (see www.ftc.gov/bcp /conline/pubs/buspubs /canspam.shtm). The only email addresses you should have in your database are the ones who have "opted-in" of their own free will.

It's a fact: online newsletters (aka ezines) can further your marketing goals and get your message out to current and prospective customers in a cost-effective, credible manner. Interested parties subscribe to receive articles and informative tips from you, and it puts your business's name in front of them on a regular basis.

Newsletters are an effective way to legitimately capture the names and emails of prospective customers, so this is an important marketing tool. Once this information is entered into your database, you can offer promotions, insider information, discounted services, and more.

Provide short, interesting articles and subtly weave in a powerful marketing message. Include polls and surveys to encourage reader interaction. Quote experts in your specific industry, but note that it's generally not acceptable to sell your services in the text of the article. Use a separate ad for your sales message. You can also include affiliate links and classified ads from third-party sponsors in your newsletter.

If your newsletter offers readers information they can use, you'll get maximum readership. By educating customers and prospective clients about important senior issues, you help to make them better consumers who are more likely to use your services because they understand the value you offer. Finally, you are positioning yourself as an expert in the senior industry, which builds credibility.

Smart Tip

Shorten lengthy hyperlinks in newsletters and other publications by using TinyURL (www.tinyurl.com) or Snipr (www.snipr.com). For example, an extended link can be significantly reduced from 130+ characters to 22. These free services not only reduce the length of a URL, but can also help you manage your links by monitoring how many unique clicks they receive.

Though it's possible to manage an email list manually, it's far more efficient to automate through an autoresponder service. Many are free through discussion list forums such as Yahoo! Groups or Topica. Others are available through monthly subscription services such as Constant Contact (www.constantcontact.com) or Aweber (www.aweber .com) that come with professional templates, HTML features, and are ad-free.

Marketing
Offline for
Success

While a lot of focus is given to internet marketing to promote businesses, many prospective customers do not use the internet at all, while others are casual browsers without a lot of expertise surfing the web. There are many types of offline marketing strategies that you can use to great advantage. For maximum benefits and better exposure, integrate both traditional and online marketing efforts.

The biggest challenge you'll face as you market is that a substantial portion of your prospective clients don't even know your services are available. Partners in Caregiving is a national dementia services program created by the Robert Wood Johnson Foundation, the largest philanthropic organization in the United States solely dedicated to health and health-care issues. This program reports that less than 50 percent of households with a senior family member know about senior adult day-care programs. Unfortunately, this is true of many businesses that offer services targeting seniors, so it's important to raise public awareness about what you're doing.

When you developed your business plan, you identified the market you want to serve. Now it's time to do a little more research on that market. You know who your prospective clients are, but how can you communicate with them? Find out what publications they read, what organizations they belong to, what websites they visit, what radio stations they listen to, what television shows they watch, and what their hobbies and interests are. When you know this, you'll be able to put together a strategic marketing plan that will produce results.

Bright Idea

Turn helping clients with change-of-address notifications into a marketing tool by providing eye-catching change-of-address cards for your clients to use to announce their move to family and friends. In addition to the new address information, discreetly include your company name, a very short description of what you do (if it's not clear from your company name), your phone number, and your website to introduce your business to the card recipients.

Network, Network, Network!

Word-of-mouth will ultimately be your best and most reliable source for promoting your business. Tell everyone about your new venture—that includes family, friends, co-workers, business associates, neighbors, church members, and members of any civic, professional, or fraternal organizations you belong to. Candy Malburg says that word-of-mouth referrals for her senior massage therapy business have been one of the best forms of advertisement.

Develop relationships with physicians, operators of assisted-living facilities, hospital discharge planners, social services coordinators, geriatric case managers, managers of senior community centers, real estate agents, bankers, insurance agents, and anyone else you can think of who comes into regular contact with your target market.

"It's important to get to know different providers in your area so they will recommend your facility," says Diane Ross of Reno, Nevada-based The Continuum. "For example, when most people need an adult day-care center, they don't plan ahead; they're referred by a doctor's office or social service or senior community center."

Allen Hager of Right at Home in Omaha, Nebraska, agrees. "Most of our marketing revolves around creating relationships with people [to whom] others come for help—professional referral sources like elder law attorneys, trust officers in banks, and social workers," he says.

Join Professional Associations

Join local associations, organizations, and civic clubs, especially those affiliated with health-care services and senior communities that you can share information, resources, and services with. For example, the Healthcare Financial Management Association offers educational programs and networking opportunities in more than 70 chapters across the United States. Find out when your local chamber of commerce, Rotary Club, or Toastmasters group holds meetings that you can attend and exchange business cards with new acquaintances.

Dick Padgett of San Diego's Five Star Concierge says that personal networking is one of the best marketing tools. His membership in two local networking groups, North Coast Business Network (NCBN) and Serving Seniors Networking Breakfast (SSNB), has generated a substantial amount of business. "We refer clients to each other's businesses. I think I have worked for every single person in NCBN, doing things they don't want—or have time—to do. The SSNB has provided several referrals to seniors who need my services. So I have gotten a lot of business that way," he says. If your community doesn't have a networking group like this, consider starting one. Also look into the Better Business Bureau and your local Chamber of Commerce for leads.

Hager suggests that one of the first things a new business owner do is join the local chamber of commerce or other small-business networking group. He says there is a wealth of information you can learn from small-business owners in other industries who have successfully carved out a niche for themselves.

Speaking Engagements and Seminars

Hit the "rubber chicken circuit" and make yourself available as a speaker to every professional, fraternal, and service organization in

Bright Idea

Most people think of themselves as 10 to 20 years younger than their actual age. Keep this in mind when developing your marketing messages, and use images of people to whom your prospective clients can relate.

▲

town. Many of these groups meet weekly, and they are always looking for speakers. You won't get paid, but you'll get a free meal, make some valuable contacts, and get the word out about your business. Judith Heft says when she first started her bill paying and administrative services for seniors, she promoted her business by speaking at various senior organizations.

Develop a 30- to 45-minute presentation about an aspect of the services you provide. Keep the information you provide helpful, but general—don't make this a sales pitch for your company. Provide images to show on PowerPoint slides; however,

---

To Publish or Not to Publish

Printed newsletters can further your company's marketing goals and get your message out to current and prospective customers in a cost-effective, credible manner. Candy Malburg says that placing newsletters and informational sheets in residents' mailboxes or distributing them around retirement communities has been a great marketing strategy. Here are some tips to get you started:

Be sure your newsletter really is a newsletter, not just a monthly sales brochure. Give readers information they can use, not just about your company, but about your industry. Then explain how that affects your customers.

Provide short, interesting, magazine-style articles and subtly weave in a powerful marketing message. Include checklists and tests that encourage reader interaction. Quote experts—even experts from your own company—to make your point, but never attempt to sell your service in the text of the article. Use a separate ad for your sales message.

If your newsletter offers readers information they can use, you'll get maximum readership. By educating your clients and prospective clients about important issues, you make them better consumers who are more likely to buy from you because they understand the value you offer. Finally, you are positioning yourself and your company as experts, and this builds credibility.

Just because you are good at what you do and happen to have a computer doesn't mean you can create an effective newsletter. If necessary, hire experienced professionals to write and produce your newsletter. To find someone, ask for referrals among your business associates. Call local publications and ask the editor to recommend a good freelance writer; then ask the writer about a design and layout person. Or check your local Yellow Pages under "Graphic Artists," "Newsletters," or "Writers."

---

obtain required releases from the persons and items in the photos before using them. A multimedia seminar is more engaging and memorable to the audience. Have business cards and brochures or some other useful handout to distribute at the end of your presentation. For example, moving management specialist Karen Martin in Hartford, Connecticut, gives talks on

> ### Bright Idea
> Check with churches in your market area to see if they have senior groups that you may be able to speak to about your services.

lifestyle changes as people age and the challenges of downsizing. At the end of her talk, she passes out business cards and a guide for downsizing. She says, "If they can sort through a life-time of possessions with a good support circle, great. If they can't, then they will call me. It is really important to share knowledge, and that is what I do."

Some possible topics for your presentation include coping with the stresses of caring for an aging parent at home, how to choose a retirement community, and how to help a senior stay in her own home as long as possible.

Get a list of all the organizations that might be receptive to having you speak. The chamber of commerce or public library should have this information. Send each organization a letter introducing yourself and offering your services.

If you want to do a more in-depth presentation, consider offering seminars. Seminars help your market learn to use your services more efficiently. They give you the opportunity to show, not tell, what you are all about. If someone is interested enough to attend a free half-day seminar on how to choose an adult day-care center, chances are they'll choose yours. The goodwill that comes from giving your market "something for nothing" is immeasurable and will go a long way toward building client loyalty.

Community Events and Trade Shows

Community events, trade shows, and conferences can be a tremendous opportunity for learning—or a huge waste of time. Malburg says that participating in health fairs has been an effective marketing strategy for her business.

Consider hosting a exhibition booth at a farmer's market or local mall. Invite visitors to fill out an information card to enter a raffle for a prize such as a first-aid kit, dinner, or something related to your business. Then, follow up later with the new lead by sending more information about you and your business.

When it comes to trade shows, there are two basic styles of shows: an exhibition, where companies set up booths to display their products and services, and an educational conference, which consists of training sessions in a variety of formats. Many show sponsors combine the formats for a broader appeal.

While local consumer shows can provide a tremendous amount of exposure at a relatively low cost, trade shows can be expensive to participate in. However, you can benefit from exhibiting in shows that specifically target seniors.

To find out about local events and trade shows in your area, call your local chamber of commerce or convention center and ask for a calendar.

Bright Idea

To get your concierge or transportation business off the ground, offer to run the first errand within a five- to ten-mile radius for free.

When you've identified potential events, contact the host or sponsor for details. Find out who will attend—promoters should be able to estimate the total number of attendees and give you demographics so you can tell if they fit your target market profile.

Attend several events or shows before you exhibit to get a solid sense of how they work and how you can best benefit from them. Once you make the decision to exhibit, give plenty of thought to the setup of your booth. Your exhibit does not need to be elaborate or expensive, but it does need to be professional and inviting. Even though the event sponsors may provide one, do not put a table across the front of your exhibit space; that creates a visual and psychological barrier that will discourage visitors from coming in. Consider an interactive demonstration that will encourage people to stop for more information. For example, a home health-care operator could have a nurse at the booth to take blood pressure or conduct cholesterol checks.

Your signage should entice clients and list your company name. For example, if you operate a senior travel business, the prominent words on your sign might be "Come Sail Away with Us!" and then your company's name.

Arrange for sufficient staffing so your booth is never unattended during exhibit hours. You don't want to miss out on even one sales opportunity. Also, it would be easy for someone to walk off with valuable items if you're not there.

Consider giveaway items such as pens, mugs, or notepads imprinted with your company name. Don't display these items openly; doing so will only crowd your booth with "trade show tourists" who are not really prospective clients. Instead, store them discreetly out of sight and present them individually when appropriate. Be sure you have an adequate stock of brochures, business cards, and perhaps discount coupons or a special offer for show attendees.

Business Cards

As small as they are, business cards are a powerful marketing tool. Hand out these little gems at every opportunity. Business cards are mini-billboards that tell people who you are, what you do and how to reach you. Even if you do the majority of your business online, you still need to have business cards on hand.

Whenever you meet someone—in church, at your kids' school, in the grocery store, waiting in lobbies, at business meetings, or anywhere else—and the subject of what you do for a living comes up, hand over your business card as you describe your company. Your own business cards in your own wallet are a waste of money; they don't begin to work for you until they're in someone else's hands. You never know who will need your services or know someone else who does, and you want to be sure they remember your name and know how to reach you.

A quick-print shop can do a nice, affordable job on your business cards and provide a variety of templates to choose from. You can also design and print them yourself on your computer or order them from an online company.

Advertising and Public Relations

Advertising and public relations are the two key ways you'll communicate the details of your business to the public. Where and how you choose to advertise will depend on your budget and your goals.

Yellow Pages

Using directory advertising, such as the Yellow Pages of the local phone book, is an important marketing tool that is often overlooked. Believe it or not, people actually use these tomes for more than doorstops and birdcage liners. When a prospective customer is looking for specific senior services in the directory, they are an excellent prospect because they are actively looking for your type of business.

Placing your listing in the right category is critical so people can find you. You will also increase the chances of a potential client seeing your business if you insert your listing under multiple headings or categories.

Karen Martin says that using the online Yellow Pages (yellowpages.com) has also been an effective marketing tool for her business.

Magazine and Publication Ads

Magazine and publication ads are effective, but they are sometimes expensive and can be hard to get responses from unless they are carefully crafted with an explicit call to action. That's usually achieved by promoting a specific product, service or information. Add an incentive such as a discount if a client contacts you and mentions seeing the advertisement, or include a coupon as part of your display ad.

Use niche publications that match your business. For instance, an independent travel agent can publicize to affinity groups that might be found through a history or travel magazine or newsletter. Advertising in local newspapers is another excellent way to create public awareness of your business.

Direct Mail

Because of the ability to target well-defined geographical areas, direct mail can be an effective way to promote your services for seniors. It also allows you to send a personalized sales message. Doug Iannelli of Atlanta, Georgia says that he has found direct mail to be an effective marketing strategy to let seniors know about his services. "It's not inexpensive to do a professional mailing," he says. "But I find that seniors will hold onto my direct mail piece until they need my services—and then they call."

There is no magic formula when using direct mail, except that using a solo mailer is more successful than including your information in a cooperative mailer full of supermarket coupons. Depending on what your services are, you can send a flashy postcard, informative brochure, or a sales letter with a personal touch.

Statistically, a 1 percent direct mail response rate is considered excellent, so if you mail 1,000 pieces and receive 10 phone calls, that's a great turnaround. Mailing lists can be purchased from list brokers, which you can find in your Yellow Pages under "Advertising—Direct Mail." These lists come in just about every category, and since you've done your marketing homework, you already know the lists you want. The one-time rental fee for these names is between $35 and $50 per thousand, with a minimum rental of 5,000 names.

Dick Padgett also uses direct mail to market his business. Check out the brochure on page 189 that he sends out to promote Five Star Concierge. Add value to your direct mailer by presenting some sort of bonus offer such as a discount or coupon. This can be an excellent way to generate business.

Press Releases

Press releases are free publicity spots that expose your business to the community; but to be printed in the news, the information in your release has to be newsworthy. One way this subtle form of self-promotion can be done is by tying the announcement into local or national events, community programs, or holidays, such as Older Americans Month or Grandparents Day.

Sample Brochure

A brochure can be an effective marketing tool that can help you sell your services and continue selling them when you're not around. When designing your brochure, keep your market in mind: Make it appealing and easy to read, use simple fonts, and don't clutter it up with unnecessary graphics. Clearly state your services and the benefits to your clients. Most important, be sure your contact information is prominently positioned. The following brochure that Dick Padgett developed for Five Star Concierge in San Diego is a good example of an effective brochure:

Inside Flap   Back Cover   Front Cover   Inside Flap

Inside Spread

Make Contact with Coupons

If you're not feeling altogether flush, a viable direct-mail alternative is a coupon mailer that groups retail businesses within a community together in a bound coupon book usually including advertisements, discounts, or special offers. The books are mailed nonselectively to all homes within a specific zip code, so they aren't as targeted as a direct-mail piece that you'd design yourself, but they can still have great pull. As a business owner, you pay a fee to the company producing and distributing the coupon books; these companies should be listed in your Yellow Pages.

Make up a list of media contacts including television, radio, newspaper, and community organizations so that when you are ready, you can plan a press release blitz. Be sure to include your contact information, including your cell phone number. Folks in the media work on tight deadlines, and if they can't reach you right away to ask questions, they may be inclined to drop the story and move on to another one.

Television/Radio

Television and radio can be effective in your marketing strategy if you're advertising something concrete, like a seasonal promotion or a special event. It also helps if you're advertising locally, where you know potential customers are listening to your chosen station.

While these stations only reach very small geographic areas, their programs are specifically designed to appeal to the people in this limited market. When you buy time on a small radio or cable TV station, you're not paying for wasted circulation. Rates are usually pretty reasonable, and you can create your own interesting, affordable ad.

Be sure to ask every client and prospective client how they heard about you so you can track the effectiveness of your efforts. Fliers, brochures, and newsletters are all excellent ways to get the word out about your business. Check out the sample flier on page 191 for an example.

Final Tips

Here are some final thoughts on marketing your senior service business:

Sample Flier

Driving Miss Daisy
Senior Transportation Service

- Door-to-door service for:
  - Medical appointments
  - Shopping trips
  - Adult day centers
  - Recreational activities
  - Community & church functions
  - Banking needs

- Affordable rates
- Comfortable ride
- Wheelchair ramp
- Licensed, insured & friendly drivers
- Will gladly escort and stay with client for duration of trip

Service available for the entire Tri-County area.

Call: (555) 987-6543

Senior Transportation Service (555) 987-6543 · Senior Transportation Service (555) 987-6543 · Senior Transportation Service (555) 987-6543 · Senior Transportation Service (555) 987-6543 · Senior Transportation Service (555) 987-6543 · Senior Transportation Service (555) 987-6543 · Senior Transportation Service (555) 987-6543 · Senior Transportation Service (555) 987-6543 · Senior Transportation Service (555) 987-6543 · Senior Transportation Service (555) 987-6543

- *Be sure every marketing message you create is complete.* It must tell prospects who you are, what you do, and how they can become your clients.

- *Always be on the lookout for marketing opportunities.* They'll pop up when you least expect them, so be ready to take advantage of them when they do.

- *Don't reinvent the wheel.* Look at what other successful companies have done—even those in businesses totally unrelated to yours—and adapt their strategies to your company and circumstances.

- *Be a visible member of your target market's community.* Prospective clients will remember that you participated in community events much longer than they'll remember an advertisement.

- *Monitor all your marketing programs.* Keep track of what you're doing, what it costs, and what the results are. Make changes when necessary. Do more of what works, and stop doing what isn't paying off.

Tom Mann of TR Mann Consulting says that not all seniors are alike. "Marketers need to understand that it's about 'stage,' not age," he says. "In other words, where is the individual in their personal journey?" An example he uses comes from one of his clients, *GRAND* magazine. The magazine doesn't address the readers' age; it addresses the stage of life this group (grandparents) has just entered. By recognizing the importance of the grandparents' role, *GRAND* and its advertisers connect with their audience on a deeper level. "Think about it this way," Mann says. "There are over 72 million grandparents in America, and according to Age Wave Communications they'll spend over $30 billion this year on their grandchildren."

17

Financial Matters

There are two key sides to the issue of money: how much you need to start and operate, and how much you can expect to take in. Doing this analysis is often extremely difficult for small-business owners who would rather be in the trenches getting the work done than bound to a desk dealing with tiresome numbers. But force yourself to do it anyway.

One of the primary indicators of the overall health of your business is its financial status, and it's important that you monitor your financial progress closely. The only way you can do that is to keep good records. There are a number of excellent computer accounting programs on the market; another option is to handle the process manually. Ask an accountant for assistance getting your system set up. The key is to do that from the beginning and keep your records current and accurate for the life of your company.

The first step is to open a separate checking account for your business so that you don't commingle personal and business funds. Next, get a business credit card or at least a separate card in your name that you use exclusively for your senior services business. Charging business expenses eliminates the risk of losing receipts for cash purchases. If you carry a balance on a credit card that is used solely for business purposes, the interest is deductible, but if you mix business and personal charges on the card, the interest is not even partially deductible.

You will also want to set up a separate filing cabinet exclusively for business use. A good plan is to set up files by year so it's easy to pull information out by date if necessary. Have separate files for clients, payroll, payables, and receivables.

Keeping good records helps generate the financial statements that tell you exactly where you stand and what you need to do next. The key financial statements you need to understand and use regularly are:

- *Profit and loss statement* (also called the P&L or the income statement), which illustrates how much your company is making or losing over a designated

The Tax Man Cometh

Businesses are required to pay a wide range of taxes, and there are no exceptions for senior services business owners. Keep good records so you can offset your local, state, and federal income taxes with the expenses of operating your company. Be sure you charge, collect, and remit appropriate sales tax on your products and services. If you have employees, you'll be responsible for payroll taxes. If you operate as a corporation, you'll have to pay payroll taxes for yourself; as a sole proprietor, you'll pay self-employment tax. Then there are property taxes, taxes on your equipment and inventory, fees, and taxes to maintain your corporate status, your business license fee (which is really a tax), and other lesser-known taxes. Take the time to review all your tax liabilities with your accountant.

period—monthly, quarterly, or annually—by subtracting expenses from revenue to arrive at a net result, which is either a profit or a loss.

- *Balance sheet*, which is a table showing your assets, liabilities, and capital at a specific point. A balance sheet is typically generated monthly, quarterly, or annually when the books are closed.

- *Cash flow statement*, which summarizes the operating, investing, and financing activities of your business as they relate to the inflow and outflow of cash. As with the profit and loss statement, the cash flow statement reflects a specific accounting period, such as monthly, quarterly, or annually.

Successful small-business owners review these reports regularly, at least monthly, so they always know where they stand and can quickly correct minor difficulties before they become major financial problems. If you wait until November to figure out whether you made a profit last February, you won't be in business long.

Both Dick Padgett and Karen Martin monitor the status of their businesses by using the QuickBooks software accounting system. Martin says, "It is a very efficient way of recording all the expenses and income into specific categories. It makes life a lot easier." Padgett adds that the software helps him keep track of clients that he adds or loses, as well as how much business he does for each client. It's also helpful when using independent contractors because you need to keep meticulous account of your contractor expenses and file annual 1099s with the government.

Sources of Startup Funds

How much money you need to start depends on the type of business you're going to open, if you are homebased or have a commercial facility, how much equipment you need, whether you buy new or used, your inventory, your marketing, and your operating capital needs (the amount of cash you need on hand to carry you until your business begins generating income). It's easy to spend hundreds of thousands of dollars starting a new business, but you could also be operating with an investment of just a few hundred dollars.

Regardless of how much, you will need cash to start your senior services business. Here are some suggestions of where to go to raise your startup funds:

- *Your own resources.* Do a thorough inventory of your assets. People generally have more assets than they realize. This could include savings accounts, equity in real estate, retirement accounts, vehicles, recreation equipment, collections, and other investments. You may opt to sell assets for cash or use them as loan collateral. For example, when Dick Padgett started his transportation business in San Diego, he used the equity in his car as a down payment for a new van. Take a look, too, at your personal line of credit. Many a successful business has been started with credit cards.

- *Family and friends.* The logical next step after gathering your own resources is to approach friends and relatives who believe in you and want to help you succeed. Be cautious with these arrangements; no matter how close you are, present yourself professionally, put everything in writing, and be sure the individuals you approach can afford to take the risk of investing in your business.

- *Partners.* Using the "strength in numbers" principle, look around for someone who may want to team up with you in your venture. You may choose someone who has financial resources and wants to work side-by-side with you in the business. Or you may find someone who has money to invest but no interest in doing the actual work. Create a written partnership agreement that clearly defines your respective responsibilities and obligations.

- *Government programs.* Take advantage of the abundance of local, state, and federal programs designed to support small businesses. Make your first stop the SBA; then investigate various other programs. Women, minorities, and veterans should check out niche financing possibilities designed to help them get into business. The business section of your local library is a good place to begin your research. Diane Ross of Reno, Nevada's The Continuum says that in hindsight, it would have been better if she had purchased the facility for her adult day-care center instead of leasing it so that she could have applied for an SBA loan.

- *Lending institutions.* While a bank might seem like the most likely source of financing, they are generally the most conservative. Besides wanting to know exactly what the money is for (show them your business plan), they usually require some type of collateral such as real estate, a life insurance policy, stocks, bonds, or a savings account. If you have excellent credit you may be able to take out a signature loan for a few thousand dollars; although the interest rate will be higher than a traditional loan.

Getting Paid

How will your clients pay you? That depends, of course, on your specific business. Travel services are usually pay-as-you-go, but other senior services use a combination of billing and collecting when the service is provided. Decide how you're going to get paid and establish clear and appropriate policies that are fair to your clients and protect you.

If you are extending credit to your clients, decide when payments are due and make that a clear part of your policy statement. For late payments, consider taking an approach similar to this: Send late notices when the payment is two days late. If payment is not made within a week, speak to the client or caregiver by phone or the next time you see them. Your policy should also address how far an account may be in arrears before you suspend services to that client until full payment is made. This is always a tough call, especially when you're dealing with seniors who may have limited resources. But remember that you are a for-profit business, and if you don't get paid, you can't pay your own bills and make a profit.

> ### Smart Tip
>
> If possible, bill at the time services are rendered. That's when the appreciation of your work is highest: When clients are thinking about you in a positive way, they're likely to process your invoice faster.

You'll also want to establish a schedule of late fees and charges for bad checks. For example, you could charge $15 per day for late payments and a one-time fee of $30 if a check bounces. Make sure clients or their caregivers are aware of these policies when they sign up for your services, and give them a copy of the fees and charges in writing so there is no question later on.

While you have a right to expect to be paid on time for your services, you might also want to consider ways to make it easy for clients to pay on schedule. For example, your payment schedule may not match their needs. Some clients will find it more convenient to pay you once a month on the day they receive Social Security, pension, or other payments; others will prefer to pay weekly; and others every other week. If you are having payment problems with a particular client, find out if a different payment schedule would solve the problem. While this may be a little more work for you in terms of bookkeeping, it will probably be less of a problem than being paid late every week.

> ### Beware!
>
> Including fliers or brochures with your invoices is a great marketing tool, but remember that adding an insert may cause the envelope to require extra postage. Certainly getting out the marketing message is probably well worth the extra few cents in mailing costs; just be sure you check the total weight before you mail so your invoices aren't returned to you for insufficient postage—or worse, delivered "postage due."

The bulk of your payments will likely come in on the same day each week, and you should keep this in mind as you plan your record-keeping tasks. Schedule other administrative tasks, such as handling payables and payroll, for days when you won't have a heavy influx of payments.

Most bookkeeping software programs include a basic invoicing function that will be sufficient for your business. If you choose to design your own invoices and statements, be sure they're clear and easy to understand. Detail each item, and indicate the amount due in bold with the words "Please pay" in front of the total. A confusing invoice may be set aside for clarification, and your payment will be delayed.

Finally, use your invoices as marketing tools. Add a flier or brochure to the envelope—even though the invoice is going to an existing client, you never know where your brochures will end up.

Accepting Credit and Debit Cards

Many of today's consumers prefer to pay with plastic, whether for convenience, security, reward points, or out of habit. Clients you bill on a regular basis may appreciate the convenience of having their credit cards automatically charged each month so they don't have to write a check—and that also means you don't have to wait to get paid.

> **Bright Idea**
> On your contract, include a statement describing the methods of payment (cash, specific credit cards, checks) you accept. That way clients won't be surprised when they try to pay with a method you do not accept.

Most small-business owners find it helps if they are able to accept credit and debit cards. It's much easier to get merchant status than it has been in the past; in fact, these days merchant status providers are competing aggressively for your business.

To get a credit card merchant account, start with your own bank. Also check with various professional associations that offer merchant status as a member benefit. Shop around; this is a competitive industry, and it's worth taking the time to get the best deal.

Accepting Checks

Although paying by plastic is a popular trend, in a senior services business, many of your clients will prefer to write you a check. Businesses lose more than $1 billion annually because of bad checks, so look for several key items when accepting them.

Check the date for accuracy. Do not accept a check that is undated, postdated, or more than 30 days old. Be sure the written amount and numerical amount agree. Post your check acceptance procedures in a highly visible place at your facility, or in your contract or agreement. This should also include the steps you will take if a check is returned for nonpayment. Most clients understand the risks you take when accepting checks and will be willing to follow your rules.

Cash Management

One of the most overlooked capital-raising techniques is doing a better job of managing the cash you have. As obvious as the concept of efficient cash management may seem, it's often neglected because business owners underestimate how valuable it can be.

One key area of cash management is holding onto your money as long as possible by slowing down disbursements legally and fairly. For example, if an invoice is due on the 15th and you pay it on the 5th, you're losing use of those funds for 10 days and getting nothing in return.

The bottom line is not to pay anything before you have to. Even though you may have a system where you process payables on certain days, hold the checks and don't mail them until they are due.

You may also be able to negotiate longer payment terms with certain creditors. This amounts to an interest-free loan from vendors. Communicate your needs clearly. Let vendors know how they will benefit by helping you—perhaps with larger orders in the future; then be sure to honor whatever terms you agree to.

> **Tip...**
>
> **Smart Tip**
>
> You want to make a good impression when applying for a loan, and that includes presenting your company's materials in a businesslike manner. Assemble and organize all your paperwork in a professional folder or portfolio, along with any relevant brochures and price lists.

However, waiting until the last minute to pay is not always the best strategy. When negotiating terms, consider the value of early-payment discounts. If the discount is greater than your cost of borrowing money, you'll save money by paying early.

If you have a revolving line of credit, it's a good idea to talk to your banker about setting up a "sweep" account. This means the bank will automatically apply whatever cash you have on hand at the end of each business day to reduce the balance—and therefore the interest—on your loan. When checks are presented for payment, the amount is charged to your line of credit.

Ask Before You Need

Just about every growing business experiences economic rough spots and requires financing of some type sooner or later. Plan for the costs of growth and watch for signs of developing problems so you can figure out how to best deal with them before they turn into a major crisis.

Asking for money before you need it is especially important if you're going to be applying for a loan, whether it's from a private individual or a commercial loan source such as your bank. Most lenders are understandably reluctant to extend credit to a business in trouble, and if you appear desperate, you're likely to get turned down. Plan your growth and pre-sell your banker on your financial needs. Such foresight demonstrates that you are an astute business owner on top of every situation. When you do that, your chances of obtaining the funding you need, will improve significantly.

When Things
Go Wrong

Senior citizens are extremely vulnerable members of our society, and business owners and professional caregivers who work with them have a tremendous responsibility for their safety and well-being. The list of what could go wrong when a senior is in your care ranges from a minor bump or bruise to elder abuse—and includes many scenarios in between.

The first step in dealing with potentially negative situations is to be proactive and put together preventive systems to keep them from happening in the first place.

Preventing and Dealing with Injuries

When it comes to preventing and dealing with injuries, nothing replaces good judgment. Beyond that, this section discusses some practical ways to reduce or eliminate injuries while a senior is in your care, and what to do when an incident occurs.

The risk of an injury happening is directly related to the physical environment and senior clients' behaviors, and how these are managed. Injuries can be divided into two categories—unintentional and intentional. Unintentional injuries may result from choking, falls, burns, cuts, exposure to environmental hazards (such as chemicals, radon, or lead), or other accidents. Intentional injuries are usually due to negligence or abuse.

You can prevent most injuries from occurring by:

- Supervising senior clients carefully
- Installing handrails along hallways and up stairways
- Making sure there is adequate lighting in all areas
- Keeping areas free of clutter

You should also discourage your clients from doing things they are no longer able to do. For example, you may have a client who refuses to accept that his mobility has become limited; your job is to discreetly and tactfully prevent him from taking part in activities that are beyond his ability or may result in an injury.

Tip...

Smart Tip

Have emergency numbers (911, police, ambulance, and poison control center) posted by every phone. For less critical situations, have the number for "Ask a Nurse" (a common name for free telephone information services offered by local hospitals in most communities) or a similar medical reference source handy.

When an injury does occur, it requires immediate action. You will need to assess the injury to determine what type of medical attention, if any, is required. Everyone on staff should have up-to-date training in first aid and CPR. If the injury is serious, call 911 or your local emergency number. Administer any appropriate first aid or medical treatment, and notify a family member or caregiver. (See page 203 for an Emergency Information and Contact Form and page 204 for a Guardian/Caregiver Consent and Agreement for Emergencies Form.) Record all injuries on a standard form developed for that purpose. For an example, see the Injury Report Form on page 205.

Emergency Information and Contact Form

Client's name: _____

Birth date: _____

1st family member or caregiver: _____

Phone: _____ Email: _____

(cell/pager): _____

2nd family member or caregiver: _____

Phone: _____ Email: _____

(cell/pager): _____

Other emergency contacts (if family members or caregivers are not available):

Name: _____

Phone: _____ Email: _____

(cell/pager): _____

Name: _____

Phone: _____ Email: _____

(cell/pager): _____

Client's preferred sources of medical care: _____

Primary physician: _____

Address: _____

Phone: _____

Other physician: _____

Address: _____

Phone: _____

Dentist: _____

Address: _____

Phone: _____

Hospital: _____

Address: _____

Phone: _____

Ambulance service: _____

Phone: _____

(Clients or their caregivers are responsible for all emergency transportation charges.)

Client's health insurance: _____

Insurance plan: _____

ID #: _____

Group #: _____

Subscriber's name (on insurance card): _____

Special conditions, disabilities, allergies, or medical emergency information: _____

_____

Expect that injuries will occur, no matter how careful you are. And the likelihood of your senior clients becoming ill or in some way needing medical attention while in your care is strong. That's why you need first-aid kits, training, and reporting procedures. Diane Ross of The Continuum in Reno, Nevada, says her clients have been accidentally injured and become ill in her care, and the key to dealing with those situations is knowing what to do immediately. "First we will determine the extent of the injury and, if necessary, call the caregiver and even 911 if required," she says. "If the situation is serious, such as a stroke or heart attack, the procedure is to call 911 and then the caregiver."

You should have information on each client's medical care providers, including their doctor(s), dentist, and preferred hospital. There may be times when a trip to the emergency room is not necessary, but you may still need to take the client to a doctor. Or the client may be taken to the emergency room and the medical staff there finds that a consultation with the patient's primary care physician would be helpful.

Guardian/Caregiver Consent and Agreement for Emergencies Form

As caregiver/guardian, I consent to have _____ receive first aid by staff members and, if necessary, be transported to receive emergency care. I will be responsible for all charges not covered by insurance. I give consent for the emergency contact person listed below to act on my behalf until I am available. I agree to review and update this information whenever a change occurs and at least every six months.

Caregiver/guardian signature: _____

Date: _____

Caregiver/guardian signature: _____

Date: _____

Emergency contact person: _____

Address: _____

Phone: _____

Injury Report Form

Name of injured: _____

Date of injury: _____

Time of injury: _____ (A.M.) _____ (P.M.)

Sex: _____ (male) _____ (female)

Age: _____ years

Where injury happened: _____

_____

_____

How injury happened: _____

_____

_____

_____

_____

Part(s) of body injured: _____

_____

_____

Objects involved (if any): _____

_____

_____

What was done to help the injured: _____

_____

_____

_____

_____

Caregiver/guardian advised: of injury: _____ (Yes) _____ (No) to seek
medical attention: _____ (Yes) _____ (No)

Supervisor (at time of injury): _____

Person completing form: _____

Date form completed: _____

Security

Many senior adult day-care users may have some form of dementia or memory loss, such as Alzheimer's, and they require constant supervision. This creates a particular challenge for providers as they strive to ensure the safety of clients who have impaired judgment or are inclined to wander. If a care recipient is reluctant to adhere to your safety guidelines, you'll need to take some creative approaches to protect him. Use these tips to add a measure of security to your facility while still maintaining a warm, friendly atmosphere:

- *Maintain the appropriate staff-to-client ratio.* The recommended ratio should be met, which is one caregiver for every four to six clients.
- *Have a gatekeeper.* This is the person—usually the center's receptionist/secretary—in charge of screening outsiders and acting as a buffer between senior clients and the outside world. This individual should be trained on security issues and know whom to call for information or security backup, especially if a senior is adamant about leaving or if an unwanted visitor wants to come in.
- *Keep tabs.* Prevent wanderers from leaving the premises undetected by implementing safety measures such as locked doors or gates, or doors with alarms or buzzers on them that are activated when they are opened. A commercial security equipment firm can help you design an effective system.
- *Keep emergency information current.* Update your emergency information and contact form at least twice a year. Ask the client or caregivers to review what you have on file and either date and initial the form if it is still accurate or update it if it's not.
- *Communicate.* If your center is divided into separate rooms, make sure there is some form of communication immediately available among each room, the main office, and the outside world in the event of an emergency. In addition to having regular telephones in every room, intercoms, walkie-talkies, handheld radios, and cell phones are other options to consider.
- *Have floor plans of your facility available both on-site and off-site.* Physical descriptions of your building and rooms are useful in the event of any emergency and make the jobs of law enforcement and

Smart Tip

Tip...

Keep a portable first-aid kit on hand that includes a first-aid manual, assorted bandages for minor cuts and scrapes, gauze, elastic wrap, adhesive tape, antiseptic wipes, antibacterial cream, tweezers, disposable gloves, safety pins, an instant-activating cold pack, and hydrocortisone cream. Keep one of these kits in all vehicles that are used to transport seniors.

rescue personnel much easier. The plans should indicate features such as windows, doors, water shut-off valves, and electrical breaker boxes. They should also note the location of any communication devices such as televisions, telephones, and computers.

- *Train staff to deal with volatile situations.* Staff members should know how to proceed in various situations when they are confronted with a senior client who becomes angry and/or aggressive.
- *Maintain copies of emergency contact information off-site.* In emergency situations, names and phone numbers of family members and caregivers become critical. Who is in and out of the building is also important information that should be available from a secure location in case the office is not accessible for any reason.

When You Suspect Abuse

Anyone who works with seniors is required by law to report abuse when they see evidence or have reasonable suspicion that an elderly person is being mistreated. Each state defines abuse in its statutes, and while those definitions differ somewhat, most contain the following elements:

- *Emotional abuse.* This consists of acts that damage a senior in psychological ways but do not fall into other categories of abuse. For prosecution, most states require that psychological damage be very definite and clearly diagnosed by a psychologist or psychiatrist; this category of abuse is rarely reported and even more rarely a cause of protective action.

- *Neglect.* General neglect is a failure to provide the common necessities, including food, shelter, a safe environment, and health care, but without resultant or likely harm to the senior. Severe neglect is neglect that results or is likely to result in harm to the elderly person.

- *Physical abuse.* This is an intentional act affecting a person that produces tangible physical harm. Whether or not you are required to do so by law, take photographs for your own files of any injuries that may be the result of abuse.

Stat Fact
According to statistics obtained from the National Center on Elder Abuse (NCEA), between 1 and 2 million Americans age 65 or older have been injured, exploited, or otherwise mistreated by someone on whom they depended for care or protection. Experts believe that only one in five cases of elder abuse is reported because victims are too afraid or embarrassed to file a complaint.

- *Sexual abuse*. This is any sexual act performed with a senior by someone who exerts control over the victim. (Many state laws provide considerable detail about the specific acts that constitute sexual abuse.)
- *Financial abuse*. This type of abuse is the hardest to see, and often it is not detected until it is too late to recover financial loss. Financial abusers can be strangers who try to scam the elderly by soliciting contributions or doing bogus home repairs, or caregivers or family members who have access to the senior's financial records.

If you suspect elder abuse, your local Adult Protective Services or police department will instruct you on the steps to take. Have a system set up as part of your policies and procedures so everyone in your company knows what to do if they suspect a client is being abused in any way.

Negative Publicity

No matter how well you prepare, there will be situations beyond your control and problems you can't avoid. You will need plans in place to deal with problems.

A key element of your plan should be what to do if a crisis occurs and the media get involved. Even a minor situation can snowball into a publicity nightmare if handled improperly.

What might prompt unfavorable media coverage? Circumstances could include a senior who wanders off, an injury to an elderly client, a traffic accident when transporting seniors, or any situation where you and your business are inadvertently thrust into the spotlight. Once started, negative publicity can be fueled by competitors, disgruntled employees, or unhappy clients.

Smart Tip

You may find it beneficial to hire an outside public relations expert who can help you develop a public relations plan and run interference if a problem arises.

If you and your business come under fire, try to avoid "no comment" responses, which may only amplify negative viewpoints. If you don't know the answer to the questions being asked at that time, say so and tell the reporter or interviewer that you will research it and get back to her. Otherwise, answer honestly and forthrightly about what happened and explain that you intend to handle the situation. Always protect your clients' privacy.

Designate one individual as the company spokesperson. Everyone on your staff should know who that person is and refer any media inquiries to that person. Your spokesperson should have some experience dealing with the media and should know how to answer questions without creating legal liability.

Tales from the
Trenches

By now, you should know how to get started

and have a good idea of what to do—and what not to do—in

your own senior service business. But nothing teaches as well

as the voice of experience. So we asked established business

owners to tell us what has contributed to their success. Here's

what they had to say.

▲

Advertise with Caution

Allen Hager, owner and founder of Right at Home in Omaha, Nebraska, cautions new business owners not to waste a lot of money on advertising. In his experience, direct mail is enormously expensive but does not usually produce results proportionate to the cost. The same can be said for glossy magazine ads and television spots. "It is very seductive, because it looks good," says Hager. "And I'm not saying that all advertising is bad; I just think a huge amount is wasted or misplaced." Carefully evaluate opportunities and spend your advertising dollars wisely.

Hager, who is a proponent of networking, says, "Most of our marketing really revolves around creating relationships with people that others come to for help; professional referral sources like elder law attorneys, trust officers in banks, and social workers."

R-E-S-P-E-C-T

Anya Clowers of Jet With Comfort feels that it's important to have great respect for our older population and value the wisdom they have. "Never underestimate someone who is elderly," she advises. "Seniors have valuable life experience they can share with you." Clowers feels that it must be difficult to be elderly in today's world with the lack of work ethic, patriotism, and respect from younger generations. She has found that her crabbiest patients were also the ones who were the most scared and feeling out of control. "I think this is another thing to keep in mind with the elderly population," she says. "It is a scary economic world and for someone on a fixed income—this can be terrifying."

Get an Early Start!

Candy Malburg says that many of the seniors she works with fill their days with activities. She makes it a point to call early in the day so she can catch them before they are off and running. "I generally schedule appointments with clients in the morning so they can make it to lunch appointments and afternoon activities without feeling rushed," she says.

Malburg also advises unblocking your phone because many people will not answer the phone if they cannot identify the caller. This can sometimes be a problem if you are calling from a cell phone. "I have a client who will not answer the phone if she doesn't see the name," Malburg says. "So I always have to remember to call her from my office phone so that she can see it is me."

Don't Take Every Job

Avoid overextending yourself. Don't take on more jobs or assignments than you can handle or accept projects that you are not qualified to do. If you are asked to do a job that is beyond your expertise or skills, let the client know that you are unable to perform that service. For example, when asked to do something special, tell customers you are not a contractor and cannot perform remodeling or renovation projects. Be honest and upfront with your customers and don't be afraid to refer them to someone else, if necessary. You'll be doing the right thing for your client, and it's likely that the person you refer to will return the favor later on.

Also, if you can't make money on a job or if the work is undesirable for any reason, turn it down. It's better to focus your time and energy on profitable work you enjoy.

Have Realistic Expectations

Allen Hager says that if he were starting his business today, he would change his expectations. "I went in with some delusions of grandeur," he says, thinking he would have a profitable business within a few months. Fortunately, he was prepared for the financial shortfall, but many new business owners are not. "Miracles happen," he says, "but that doesn't usually pay the rent. It's a scary thing for families when they're suddenly three or six months into the business and they haven't made any money yet and are wondering what they're going to do."

Be realistic when forecasting your cash flow, and have enough startup capital available to get you through even longer than you think you'll need.

Watch for Warning Signs

Don't be fooled into thinking a senior client might not be "the sharpest tool in the shed." Although memory may decline with age, judgment often significantly improves. It's also important to know that sometimes symptoms such as confusion, disorientation, or hallucinations are mistaken for senility. However, these conditions can also result from depression, congestive heart failure, medications, an infection, or a number of other causes. If yours is a home care or senior adult day-care center, staff members should be properly trained to recognize warning signs that something might be amiss. Have procedures in place so the family caregiver or physician can be notified right away. Diane Ross, owner and founder of The Continuum in Reno, Nevada, says her new day-care employees shadow a medical staff member so they can learn some of the red flags to watch out for that indicate a senior client could be in distress.

Communicate Clearly

Clear communication can sometimes be a challenge when you're dealing with seniors. Don't assume your clients will remember everything you have told them. Karen Martin, the Hartford, Connecticut, moving management specialist recommends having a family member or friend on hand to assist in the communication process. She puts everything in writing and makes sure that her contracts spell out what she will and will not do, and cautions, "You have to be clear in disclosing how you operate so there are no disappointments or misunderstandings." Martin also advises that it's important to have the proper "release clauses" in your contract to protect your company.

Though moving is a job for her, she recognizes that downsizing and relocating can be an emotional and even painful time for her clients, and the result can be misunderstandings and even anger. "I think that the grief triggers a displacement of their feelings, and anybody in this business can be a target for uncomfortable situations to arise," she says. Martin's book, *Gaining Control Over Home Downsizing: Inspirational Stories*, published in April 2007, was written to help people gain insight into the enormous task of leaving a long-time home. In the midst of their downsize moves, her clients wanted others to learn from their experiences and graciously agreed to tell their true story.

Just Say "No"

There may be times when a client will ask you to do something you are uncomfortable doing. When that happens, don't hesitate to say "no." Of course, it will help if you are clear about your position from the start. You can do that by attaching a list of available services to the contract. If you have a concierge service and there are things you will not do or products you will not purchase, discreetly note that on your service list. For example, you may prefer not to purchase alcohol, cigarettes, or items considered "adult products" for your clients. If you have indicated this ahead of time, and a client asks you to do something you're not comfortable with, simply refer to the service list and politely decline.

Document Everything

Because you never know what kind of questions may arise and when, document all your communications and everything you do with and for your clients and their families. Karen Martin says her nursing background of taking copious notes and keeping accurate documentation has helped in this regard. "Whether it's phone calls, emails, or conversations that you have had with someone," she advises, "take notes and include the time, the date, the person, the particular incident or problem, and any resolution, so that in the future if anything arises, you have protection."

Be Prepared for Surprises

Sometimes inappropriate or erratic behavior by a senior may indicate that he is experiencing some health-related problems. For instance, if Gramps becomes enamored and somewhat frisky with an aide, it may be a sign of advancing senility. If the client has suffered a stroke or has Alzheimer's, he may even believe the recipient of his affection is someone from another time in his life who would welcome his advances. Of course, this type of conduct needs to be immediately halted, but it should be done with tact and grace. It may require a frank discussion with the client's family or caregiver, especially if it becomes a persistent problem. His physician will also need to be alerted to any changes, whether physical or mental.

Outperform the Competition

There is always room for improvement, so if you see your competition doing something that works and you like the idea, do it—and do it better. When Dick Padgett of San Diego's Five Star Concierge started his business, he found that his competition offered a four-hour minimum service, which was often more than people needed. "Sometimes people only need an hour or half-hour worth of your time, so I decided that I would bill in 15-minute increments with a minimum based on how long it takes me to get to the client's door; sometimes as little as ½ hour," he says.

There are many ways that you can outperform your competition. Sometimes it's just as simple as offering better customer assistance, a money-back guarantee, or 24-hour emergency service. Competitive prices are also a factor, but if your rates are higher, find out how you can raise the perceived value of your services so that people will think they are getting more for their money.

It's Like a Vacation

Allen Hager says that preparing to start a new business is a lot like preparing to go on a vacation. "There is an old adage about vacationing that I think has a lot to do with opening a business," he says. "First, you get together all the clothes and other things you want to take and get the money you think you will need from the bank. Then you put back half your clothes and belongings and go back to get twice as much money from the bank, and you're ready to go!"

The Bottom Line

Is operating a business that serves the elderly population for you? Only you can make that call. For those cut out for one of these types of businesses, working with seniors can be exciting, challenging, rewarding—and profitable.

The bottom line is that one size does not fit all. You can decide whether your goal is to generate occasional part-time income working by yourself from home or to build a substantial operation with commercial facilities and employees—or something in between. If this sounds like your cup of tea, what are you waiting for?

Appendix
Senior Care Resources

They say you can never be too rich or too thin. While these could be argued, we believe you can never have too many resources. Therefore, we present for your consideration a wealth of sources for you to check into, check out and harness for your own personal information blitz.

These sources are tidbits—ideas to get you started on your research. They are by no means the only sources out there, and they should not be taken as the Ultimate Answer. We have done our research, but businesses move, change, fold, and expand. As we have repeatedly stressed, do your homework. Get out there and start investigating.

Associations, Education, and Certification Organizations

AAA Foundation for Traffic Safety
607 14th St. NW, #201
Washington, DC 20005
(202) 638-5944, Fax: (202) 638-5943
aaafoundation.org

Alzheimer's Association National Office
225 N. Michigan Ave., 17th Fl.
Chicago, IL 60601
(800) 272-3900
alz.org

American Association for Homecare
1707 L Street NW, Ste. 350
Washington, DC 20036
(202) 372-0107, Fax: (202) 835-8306
aahomecare.org

American Association of Retired Persons
601 E St. NW
Washington, DC 20049
(888) 687-2277
aarp.org

American Business Women's Association
11050 Roe Ave., Ste. 200
Overland Park, KS 66211
(800)228-0007
abwa.org

American Council on Exercise
4851 Paramount Dr.
San Diego, CA 92123
(800) 825-3636
acefitness.com

American Errand Runners Organization
errandinfo.com

American Marketing Association (AMA)
311 S. Wacker Drive, Suite 5800
Chicago, IL 60606
(800) AMA-1150 or (312) 542-9000, Fax: (312)542-9001
marketingpower.com

American Personal Chef Association
4572 Delaware St.
San Diego, CA 92116
(800) 644-8389, (619) 294-2436
personalchef.com

American Society of Travel Agents
1101 King St., #200
Alexandria, VA 22314
(800) 275-2782
asta.org

American Society on Aging
833 Market St.
San Francisco, CA 94103
(415) 974-9600, (800) 537-9728, Fax: (415) 974-0300
asaging.org

Caregiver Registry Standards Board
10685-B Hazelhurst Dr., #13776
Houston, TX 77043
www.crsbonline.com/

Continuing Care Accreditation Commission
1730 Rhode Island Ave. NW, #209
Washington, DC 20036-3120
(866) 888-1122, (202) 587-5001, Fax: (202) 587-5009
www.carf.org
An organization that compiles an annual list of "aging communities" that meet their strict criteria of standards.

Direct Marketing Association
1120 Avenue of the Americas
New York, NY 10036-6700
(212) 768-7277, Fax: (212) 302-6714
the-dma.org

▲

Family Caregiver Alliance
785 Market St., Ste. 750
San Francisco, CA 94103
(800) 445-8106, (415) 434-3388
caregiver.org

Healthcare Financial Management Association
3 Westbrook Corporate Center, #600
Westchester, IL 60154-5700
(800) 252-4362, Fax: (708) 531-0032
hfma.org

International Association for Medical Assistance to Travelers
1623 Military Rd. #279
Niagara Falls, NY 14304-1745
(716) 754-4883
iamat.org

International Concierge and Lifestyle Management Association
3650 Rogers Road, #328
Wake Forest, NC 27587
(800) 376-7020
http://iclma.org/

Leading Age
(formerly American Association of Homes and Services for the Aging)
2519 Connecticut Ave. NW
Washington, DC 20008-1520
(202) 783-2242, Fax: (202) 783-2255
wwwleadingage.org

National Adult Day Services Association
1421 E. Broad St., Ste. 425
Fuquay Varina, NC 27526
(877) 745-1440, Fax: (919) 825-3945
nadsa.org

National Association for Home Care
228 Seventh St. SE
Washington, DC 20003
(202) 547-7424, Fax: (202) 547-3540
nahc.org

National Association of Area Agencies on Aging
1730 Rhode Island Ave. NW, #1200

Washington, DC 20036
(202) 872-0888, Fax: (202) 872-0057
n4a.org

National Association of Professional Organizers
15000 Commerce Parkway, Suite C
Mount Laurel, NJ 08054
(856) 380-6828, Fax: (856) 439-0525
napo.net

National Association of Senior Move Managers
PO Box 209
Hinsdale, IL 60522
(877) 606-2766, Fax: (630) 230-3594
nasmm.com

National Center on Elder Abuse
Program in Geriatric Medicine
101 The City Drive South, 200 Building
Orange, CA 92868
(855) 500-3537, Fax: (714) 456-7933
ncea.aoa.gov

National Concierge Association
2920 Idaho Avenue North
Minneapolis, MN 55427
(612) 317-2932
www.ncakey.org/

National Council on the Aging
1901 L Street, NW, 4th Floor
Washington, DC 20036
(202) 479-1200
ncoa.org

National Notary Association
P.O. Box 2402, 9350 DeSoto Ave.
Chatsworth, CA 91311-2402
(888) 896-6827, Fax: (800) 833-1211
nationalnotary.org,

Open Doors Organization
2551 N. Clark St., #301
Chicago, IL 60614

(773) 388-8839, Fax (413) 460-5995
opendoorsnfp.org

Robert Wood Johnson Foundation
P.O. Box 2316, College Rd. E., Rte. 1
Princeton, NJ 08543
(877) 843-7953
rwjf.org

Society for Accessible Travel and Hospitality
347 Fifth Ave., #610
New York, NY 10016
(212) 447-7284, Fax: (212) 447-1928
sath.org

Travel Industry Association of America
1100 New York Ave. NW, #450
Washington, DC 20005-3934
(202) 408-8422, Fax (202) 408-1255
tia.org

The Travel Institute
148 Linden St., Ste. 305
Wellesley, MA 02482
(800) 542-4282, fax: 781-237-3860
thetravelinstitute.com

Visiting Nurse Associations of America
900 19th St, NW, Suite 200
Washington, DC 20006
(202) 384-1420, Fax: (202) 384-1444
vnaa.org

United States Personal Chef Association
610 Quantum Road, N.E.
Rio Rancho, NM 87124
(800) 995-2138
uspca.com

United States Tour Operators Association
275 Madison Ave., Ste. 2014
New York, NY 10016
(212) 599-6599, Fax (212) 599-6744
ustoa.com

Books, Magazines, and Other Publications

Aging Loved Ones: A Guide to Organizing and Managing the Aging Process, Bonnie & Norman Hardy (Hardy Wilson, 2013)

The Concierge Manual: The Ultimate Resource for Building Your Concierge and/or Lifestyle Management Company, Fourth Edition, Katharine C. Giovanni; Ron Giovanni (NewRoad Publishing, 2012)

Deduct It! Lower Your Small Business Taxes, Tenth Edition, Stephen Fishman (Nolo Press, 2013)

Gaining Control Over Home Downsizing, Karen J. Martin (Life Moves, LLC, 2007)

CDC Health Information for International Travel
Commonly called the Yellow Book, this book is published every two years by CDC with information on how travelers can protect their health, immunization advice for specific countries, and disease and health risks. Go to: wwwnc.cdc.gov/travel/page/yellowbook-home-2014 or call (800) 451-7556. Can also be ordered from major online booksellers, such as Amazon and Barnes & Noble.

How to Start a Home Based Personal Chef Business, Second Edition, Denise Vivaldo (Globe Pequot, 2011)

How to Start a Home Based Travel Agency, Tom and Joanie Ogg (CreateSpace, 2013)

Moving for Seniors: A Step-by-Step Workbook, Fifth Edition, Barbara H. Morris (Morris, 2011)

Start Up and Run Your Own Business: The Essential Guide to Planning, Funding and Growing Your New Enterprise, Eighth Edition, Jonathan Reuvid (Kogan Page, 2011)

Start Your Own Business, Fifth Edition, (Entrepreneur, 2010)

Start Your Own Cleaning Service, Third Edition, Entrepreneur Press and Jacquelyn Lynn (Entrepreneur Press, 2010)

Start Your Own Office and Administrative Support Service, Entrepreneur Press and Courtney Thurman (Entrepreneur, 2007)

Start Your Own Personal Concierge Service, Third Edition, Entrepreneur Press and Ciree Linsenman (Entrepreneur Press, 2011)

Start Your Own Personal Training Business, Third Edition, Entrepreneur Press and Cheryl Kimball (Entrepreneur Press, 2012)

Start Your Own Pet-Sitting Business, Entrepreneur Press and Cheryl Kimball (Entrepreneur Press, 2007)

Start Your Own Travel Business and More, Second Edition, Entrepreneur Press and Rich Mintzer (Entrepreneur Press, 2012)

Tax Savvy for Small Business, Twelfth Edition, Frederick W. Daily (Nolo Press, 2012)

Tradeshow Show Executive, 1945 Avenida del Oro, Suite 122, Oceanside, CA 92056-5828, (760) 630-9111, Fax: (877) 483-8912, www.tradeshowexecutive.com/

Travel For Seniors Made Easy: Staying Alive @ 65, Mike Eicher (Tate, 2013)

Walking Tour Guide Business, Roncevich & Primm (Amazon, 2011)

Consultants and Other Experts

Jacqueline (Jacke') S Dollar B.A., LHCA, LBSW, CDP
Easy Aging, Geriatric Case Management Services
West Des Moines, IA 50265
(515) 988-0041
Email: JSDx4@aol.com

Tom Mann
Managing Partner
TR Mann Consulting
(410) 292-4333
TRMann.com

Andi McClure-Mysza
President of Independent Contractor Division
Montrose Travel
2349 Honolulu Avenue
Montrose, CA 91020-1821
montrosetravel.com

Equipment, Supplies, Software, and Services

Ace Hardware
2200 Kensington Court
Oak Brook, IL 60523

(630) 990-6600
acehardware.com

Aspen Information Systems Inc.
P.O. Box 680031
Houston, TX 77268
(800) 414-0343, (281) 320-0343, Fax: (281) 251-7271
aspensoftware.com

Boxes Delivered
1030 Grand Blvd.
Deer Park, NY 11729
(866) 872-2526, Fax: (631) 667-1602
boxesdelivered.com

Creative Health Products Inc.
7621 East Joy Road
Ann Arbor, MI 48105
(800) 742-4478, (734) 996-5900, Fax: (734) 996-4650
chponline.com
Large selection of health, fitness, and rehabilitation products, equipment and books.

Home Depot
(800) 466-3337
homedepot.com

Industrial Supply
1635 S. 300 West
Salt Lake City, UT 84115
(800) 288-3838, (801) 484-8644, Fax: (801) 487-0469
indsupply.com
Safety equipment, cleaning equipment and supplies.

Lowe's Home Improvement
PO Box 1111
North Wilkesboro, NC 28656
(800) 445-6937
lowes.com

PRN Plus
OMS2 Software Inc.
4 Midland Ave., #103
Berwyn, PA 19312
(800) 279-9949
oms2.com
Home health-care software system.

▲

TimeTrack
Professional Computer Consultants Inc.
4139 Via Marina, #502
Marina del Rey, CA 90292
(888) 715-4440; fax: (310) 861-1122
time-track.com
Home health-care software system.

Franchise and Business Opportunities

The American Franchisee Association
53 West Jackson Boulevard, Suite 1256
Chicago, IL 60604
(312) 431-0545, Fax: (312) 431-1469
franchisee.org

BizBuySell
185 Berry Street, Suite 4000
San Francisco, CA 94107
(888) 777-9892, Fax: (415) 764-1622
bizbuysell.com
Useful website to find businesses for sale, as well as online tools and articles.

Comfort Keepers
CK Franchising Inc.
6640 Poe Ave., #200
Dayton, OH 45414
(937) 264-1933, (800) 477-3145, Fax: (937) 264-3103
comfortkeepers.com

Cruise Planners
(888) 582-2150
cruiseplanners.com

International Franchise Association
1501 K St. NW, Ste. 350
Washington, DC 20005
(202) 628-8000, Fax: (202) 628-0812
franchise.org

Right at Home
11949 Q St., Ste. 100
Omaha, NE 68137

▲

(877) 697-7537, Fax: (402) 697-0289
rightathome.net

General Small Business Resources

BizFilings
8025 Excelsior Drive, Ste. 200
Madison, WI 53717
(800) 981-7183, (608) 827-5300
bizfilings.com
Information on incorporating and related services for business owners, including forms, advice, and tools needed.

BPlans.com
Palo Alto Software, Inc.
44 West Broadway, Ste. 500
Eugene, OR 97401
(800) 229-7526
bplans.com
Free sample business plans, articles, and online tools.

Business Finance
909N Sepulveda Blvd 11th Floor
El Segundo, CA 90245
(800) 835-8857
businessfinance.com
Thousands of business loan and capital sources.

Business Plan Center
(800) 423-1228
businessplans.org
Sample business plans and planning guidelines for business owners.

COR-TECH HR
422 North Douty
P.O. Box 1157
Hanford, CA 93232
(800) 648-8558, Fax: (559) 582-6291
Information on writing job descriptions, HR manuals, safety tips, training resources, and more.

Entrepreneur.com
2445 McCabe Way, Ste. 400
Irvine, CA 92614
(949) 261-2325
entrepreneur.com
Tons of resources, guides, tips, articles, and more at this informative website for startup businesses and growing companies.

The Entrepreneur Institute
3700 Corporate Drive, Ste. 145
Columbus, OH 43231
(614) 895-1153
tei.net
Provides resources and networking opportunities for business owners.

Find Law for Small Business
610 Opperman Dr.
Eagan, MN 55123
(800) 455-4565, Fax: (800) 392-6206
smallbusiness.findlaw.com
Links to regulatory agencies, sample forms and contracts, articles on all aspects of business development.

The Small Business Advisor
Box 79
Great Falls, VA 22066
isquare.com
Lots of articles and advice for startup businesses.

First Data
(formerly Telecheck)
5565 Glenridge Connector NE, Ste. 2000
Atlanta, GA 30342
(404) 890-2000, (800) 735-3362
firstdata.com
Provides check-guarantee services.

Website Marketing Plan
9051 Watson Road, Suite 318
St. Louis, MO 63126
websitemarketingplan.com
Lots of informative articles, as well as sample business and marketing plans.

Government Agencies and Related Resources

Centers for Disease Control and Prevention
1600 Clifton Rd.
Atlanta, GA 30333
(800) 232-4636
cdc.gov

Department of Commerce
1401 Constitution Ave. NW
Washington, DC 20230
(202) 482-2000, Fax: (202) 482-5270
doc.gov

Department of Labor
200 Constitution Ave. NW
Washington, DC 20210
(866) 487-2365
dol.gov

Department of Veterans Affairs
810 Vermont Ave. NW
Washington, DC 20420
va.gov

Eldercare Locator
(800) 677-1116
eldercare.gov
A public service of the Administration on Aging, U.S. Department of Health and
Human Services.

Environmental Protection Agency
Ariel Rios Building
1200 Pennsylvania Ave., NW
Washington, DC 20460
(202) 272-0167
epa.gov

▲

Food and Drug Administration
10903 New Hampshire Ave.
Silver Spring, MD 20993
(888) 463-6332
www.fda.gov

Internal Revenue Service
1111 Constitution Ave. NW
Washington, DC 20224
(800) 829-4933
www.irs.gov

Library of Congress
Copyright Office
101 Independence Ave. SE
Washington, DC 20559-6000
(877) 476-0778
loc.gov/copyright

National Center for Health Statistics
1600 Clifton Rd.
Atlanta, GA 30333
(800) 232-4636
cdc.gov/nchs/

Small Business Administration
409 Third St. SW
Washington, DC 20416
(800) 827-5722
www.sba.gov

U.S. Administration on Aging
One Massachusetts Ave., NW
Washington, DC 20001
(202) 619-0724
www.aoa.gov

U.S. Business Advisor
(800) FED-INFO
www.business.usa.gov
Division of the Small Business Administration.

U.S. Department of Agriculture
1400 Independence Ave., S.W.
Washington, DC 20250

(202) 720-2791
www.usda.gov

U.S. Department of Health & Human Services
200 Independence Ave. SW
Washington, DC 20201
(877) 696-6775, (202) 619-0257
www.hhs.gov
Information on Medicare, Medicaid, and other resources

U.S. Department of Transportation
1200 New Jersey Ave., SE
Washington, DC 20590
(202) 366-4000
www.dot.gov

U.S. Postal Service
(800) 275-8777
www.usps.com

Internet Resources

American Society on Aging
asaging.org/webseminars
Free web seminars

Caregiver Resource Network
caregiverresource.net
Information on issues related to caregiving for aging individuals.

Consumer Reports
(subscription service)
consumerreports.org

ElderLifePlanning.com
elderlifeplanning.com
Directory of "Elder Care Professionals" by state.

GoDaddy
godaddy.com
Full service web solutions: domains, web hosting, site building, and SSL certificates.

Mozy
mozy.com
Online backup service

NetFirms
netfirms.com
Web hosting, domain name, ecommerce, email, emarketing services, and technology solutions.

Quantcast Internet Ratings Service
quantcast.com
This is a free service that provides audience profiles for millions of websites. A useful tool if you want to look up specific sites for advertising purposes or want to list your site so that advertisers can find you.

Register.com
register.com
Domain registration, web hosting, and email services.

Retire Net
retirenet.com
An extensive listing, by state, of various types of retirement communities and facilities.

Salary.com
salary.com
Compare salary ranges in your area with ranges in other parts of the country.

SeniorResource.com
seniorresource.com
Information on housing options, retirement, finance, insurance, and senior care.

Understanding HIPAA
www.hhs.gov/ocr/privacy/hipaa/understanding/
Information, news, and compliance stats on health information privacy.

Miscellaneous Resources

General Motors
P.O. Box 33170
Detroit, MI 48232-5170
(800) 323-9935
www.gmmobility.com/mobility-financial-assistance/
Offers financial assistance for the installation of eligible mobility equipment.

International Mature Marketing Network IMMN™
(866) 335-9777
immn.org

National Transit Database
(888) 252-0936

Travel Information Service
1200 West Tabor Road
Philadelphia, PA 19141-3099
(215) 456-9900
mossresourcenet.org/travel.htm
Moss Rehabilitation Hospital, assists handicapped or disabled travelers when planning trips domestically or abroad.

Successful Senior Service Business Owners

Anya Clowers
Jet With Comfort
Gold River, CA 95670
(916) 853-9619
JetWithComfort.com
JetWithKids.com

Allen Hager
Right at Home
11949 Q St., Ste. 100
Omaha, NE 68137
(402) 697-7537, Fax: (402) 697-0289
rightathome.net

Judy Heft
Judith Heft & Associates, LLC
Stamford, CT 06905
(203) 978-1858
judithheft.com

Douglas J. Iannelli
Appointment Companions
Flying Companions
Atlanta, GA 30324
(888) 350-8886
AppointmentCompanions.com
FlyingCompanions.com

▲

Candy Malburg
Licensed Massage Therapist
(480) 632-0248

Karen J. Martin
Life Moves, LLC
Hartford, CT
(860) 548-0002
lifemoves.com

Dick Padgett
Five Star Concierge
San Diego, CA 92130
(858) 350-7633
fivestarconcierge.org

Diane Ross
The Continuum
3700 Grant Dr., Ste. A.
Reno, NV 89509
(775) 829-4700
continuumreno.com

Glossary

Accreditation: a seal of approval given by a governing body to a housing and/or service provider.

ADA (Americans with Disabilities Act): a law passed by Congress in 1990 establishing a clear and comprehensive prohibition of discrimination on the basis of disability.

Alzheimer's disease: a progressive neurological disease that affects brain functions, including short-term memory loss, inability to reason, the deterioration of language, and the inability to care for oneself.

Area Agency on Aging: a nationwide network of programs designed to meet the needs of the elderly; services include information and referral, nutrition, employment, in-home services, counseling, and legal services.

Assessment: an in-depth appraisal conducted to diagnose a condition or determine the importance or value of a procedure.

Assisted living facility: a residential complex that accommodates senior adults by providing 24-hour care and assistance; facilities are designed to help the elderly maintain their independence and may or may not provide nursing care.

Booking: a travel reservation.

Caregiver: someone who provides assistance—usually in the home environment—to a senior adult; a caregiver may be a family member, friend, volunteer, or paid professional.

Centers for Disease Control and Prevention: an agency composed of a number of centers, institutes, and offices that aims to promote health and quality of life by preventing and controlling disease, injury, and disability.

Certification: the act of attesting that an individual or organization has met a specific set of standards.

Chronically ill: having a serious and/or persistent medical condition.

Client-to-staff ratio: the maximum number of clients permitted per caregiver or staff member.

Cognitively impaired: having a deficiency in short- or long-term memory; often affects reasoning or judgment, creating confusion and disorientation.

Companion: a person employed to assist, live with, or travel with another.

Compliance: the act of carrying out a recommendation, policy, or procedure.

Concierge: someone who performs special duties or requests on behalf of a client.

Cook date: the date the client and the personal chef have agreed the chef will come to the home to prepare meals.

Dementia: progressive neurological, cognitive, or medical disorder that affects memory, judgment, and cognitive powers, and usually interferes with daily activities.

Elder abuse: can include physical, sexual, emotional, and financial abuse, as well as neglect, abandonment, and self-neglect of an elderly person; most often it is defined as an action taken by someone who causes harm to an elderly person.

Emergency response practices: procedures used to call for emergency medical assistance, to reach family caregivers or emergency contacts, to arrange for transfer to medical assistance, or to render first aid to an injured person.

Facility: a legal definition meaning the buildings, funds, equipment, and people involved in providing senior care of any type.

General liability insurance: insurance covering the insured for bodily injury or property damage resulting from general negligence.

Grandtravel: vacations and trips that grandparents take with their grandchildren.

Handicap: physical, mental, or emotional condition that interferes with a person's normal functioning.

Handicapped-accessible: areas that are easy to get to by handicapped individuals.

Handyman: someone who does various odd jobs or small tasks.

Home care: provides a range of support services in the home to assist senior adults with daily living activities; services may include light housekeeping, companionship, medication reminders, meal preparation, personal care and grooming, errands, and transportation.

Home health care: this term covers a multitude of services, including nursing care, rehabilitation therapy, personal care, companionship, and homemaking services.

Host agency: a travel agency (with appointments to write tickets for airfare, cruise, or other travel products) through which outside or independent agents sell products.

Incontinence: inability to control excretory functions.

Independent contractor: an individual who conducts business independently on a contract basis and is not an employee of the organization or business for which they do work.

Independent travel agent: a travel agent who works alone or with a few associates or employees; usually homebased.

Kinesiology: the study of human movement.

Liability: legal responsibility for damage or injury; the responsibility is usually financial.

Medicaid: a program funded jointly by federal and state (and in some cases, city) governments for low-income people of all ages.

Medicare: a national health insurance program designed primarily for seniors age 65 and older.

Medigap insurance: a private health insurance policy that supplements Medicare coverage.

Minimum charges: the least amount you will charge, regardless of the amount of work actually done.

Occupational therapist: a rehabilitation professional who helps people compensate for cognitive and functional limitations as a result of an injury, illness, or disability; will teach skills necessary to perform functional activities of daily living and maintain independence by helping clients improve basic motor functions and reasoning abilities.

Paratransit: a specialized transportation service for persons who are unable to independently use regular public transportation due to a disability or health-related condition some or all of the time; paratransit is provided by public transportation systems as part of the requirements of the ADA.

Personal or home care aide: a person who provides services such as companionship, cooking, light cleaning, medication reminders, bathing assistance, conversation, light errands, and other in-home nonmedical care.

Personalized exercise program: an individualized exercise program based on the person's fitness evaluation results and personal fitness and health goals.

Physical therapist: a rehabilitation professional who uses different therapies to help people maximize their mobility and relieve pain; helps restore physical strength and body movement following an illness, injury, disease, or disability; and helps to prevent or limit permanent physical disabilities.

Professional liability insurance: insurance covering the insured for damages resulting from negligence, errors, or omissions.

Rehabilitation: therapeutic care for persons requiring intensive physical, occupational, or speech therapy.

Respite care: temporary or intermittent care for people with disabilities, illnesses, dementia, or other health conditions that provides relief to family caregivers; respite care can be provided at the caregiver's home, in an adult day-care center, or at an overnight facility.

Rush or emergency rates: extra charges applied to work done in less time than your standard period at the client's request.

Sandwich generation: a phrase that refers to people who have become the primary caregivers for their parents as well as their own children.

Senior adult day care: group programs that provide a secure, nurturing environment for elderly people who cannot or do not wish to be at home alone; programs are designed to meet the needs of functionally or cognitively impaired senior adults.

Senior center: a place where community-based programs provide a variety of services, including social activities and educational and recreational opportunities for senior adults.

Soft-adventure tours: involves basic accommodations, along with walking, hiking, or bicycling over terrain that is often rough and uneven, or culturally oriented activities like antiquing or gardening.

Supplier: a company that sells goods and services to other companies.

Tour operator or director: a representative who shepherds clients throughout a tour.

Turnkey service: a service provided by relocation or moving specialists where everything is unpacked, set up, and ready for the client when he or she walks into his or her new home.

Walker: a frame device used to support someone while walking.

Web host: a company that stores your website, including graphics, and transmits it to the internet for other users to view.

Index